A WESTERN JOURNEY

In memory of Denis Bowen 1921–2006
artist, inspiration and friend

A WESTERN JOURNEY

Jim Kavanagh | Richard Dyer

Arlen House | Publishers

Preface

It is a pleasure to have been asked to provide a preface to this sensuous and wonderfully worthwhile book which will go some way towards helping fund the Galway Rape Crisis Centre in its important work. The generosity of these artists, however, we must remember, should provide no absolution for the insufficiency of state funding.

It is always fascinating to observe the interplay between artists, especially artists whose metiér lie in different forms. The way in which Richard and Jim succeed in combining their fine work is exemplary and most praiseworthy. Here, the poetry does not serve to 'describe' the paintings, nor the paintings to 'illustrate' the written words. Rather, the combination of both serves to enhance the other. Two forms are stretched and the emergent combination makes a statement in its own right.

Jim's paintings are strikingly powerful. While suggestive of an underlying violence they also hint at a calmness after the storm, a light that glimmers through darkness. They are images, I feel, which are apposite for an artist working in the west of Ireland, and on a project such as this. Many of them remind us of the near infinity of the sea and the transient beauty of its interaction with the light.

His is a magnificent technique which allows these two extremes of power and tenuous peace to coexist in the same work of art. His use, also, of paints and materials shows not just the evidence of a highly original and creative mind, but of the pursuit of precision and perfection in the craft.

There is a spiritual, one might say, ethereal quality to the work. For example, the beautiful *Radharc na Todhchaí* (*Seeing the Future*), with the light breaking the dark in ripples from the centre of the picture, is evocative of the triumph of good over evil, of light over dark. Indeed, the painting's title implies that better days are to come.

Richard's poetry is sturdy, strong, and the sounds of words are pushed beyond the literal to a music out of jagged meaning. He sketches impressionistic images which swirl in the reader's head, leaving a picture that assembles and implants itself, but retains a turbulent form that promises not one response, but several.

There is a quiet insistence on the healing value of nature, and there is a good deal of loving reference to the natural, to the world which surrounds us, to the cosmos of which we are an unfulfilled part. It is, however, neither reductionism nor reactionary. The humour of the human that enables us to manage man-made modernity is also present.

The history which surrounds us, and our relationship to it, is a recurrent theme, also. The writing is dignified, and respectful: there is a sense of elegy towards the past. While one effect which one experiences while reading the poetry is that of melancholy, there is redemption, too.

As one reared in Co Clare myself, I took great pleasure in 'The Burren', a powerful piece which combines the qualities described above – the poem is rooted in nature, and portrays an intimate knowledge of the rural, depicts the way in which the past can, and does, coexist with the present, and ends on an inspiring note of rebirth and renewal.

The greatest gift artists can give is their own work, which carries their spirits, skill and craft. In this book Jim Kavanagh and Richard Dyer have created a beautiful evocation of a journey within the space that is the west of Ireland.

Michael D Higgins TD

Forward

From the Gothic-like presence of the Cliffs of Moher and the imposing grandeur of Slieve League to the sweeping heather of Achill Island and the purple mists over Leenane and Clew Bay, the west of Ireland has inspired artists for generations.

To capture something of its eerie beauty, its wilful spirit and its volatile character is a never-ending quest, but Richard and Jim cannot help but travel that long and mysterious road.

It was nearly fifteen years ago when I first saw Jim's work hanging in a central London gallery and what struck me even then was the relationship he had formed with this bewitching part of the world. His response was not to tame it, contain it or replicate it. What he wanted to do – and what he wanted us to do – was to feel it. To let this land grab you. Challenge you. Seduce you.

Like many children whose parents left Ireland in the 1950s and 1960s to settle amongst the urban sprawl of cities like London, Liverpool and Manchester, Jim's first memories of Ireland were the annual holidays to see family back home.

These were spent in and around Charleville in County Cork, a town criss-crossed by a mosaic of small country roads and bordered by the brooding presence of the Ballyhoura mountains. One imagines that, even in these early days, his artistic sensibility was already taking root.

Five years ago Jim and his wife, Annie, moved to the west – not far from where Annie was born. Their house, which sits by the shores of Lough Corrib, wakes up to a sprawling palette of colour as layer upon layer of moorland, mountain and sky battle for supremacy. On a clear day, they can see the ethereal heights of Croagh Patrick and on a black night, they can hear the wailing echoes of Mount Gable. It is a place where time stands still, and yet eternity beckons.

Like Jim, I have known Richard for many years. A distinguished art critic and poet, he too has found a calling. His own Irish ancestry and his relationship with the land and its people have stirred his mind as well as his heart. Now both of them have come together to create a book of poetry and paintings. And what an incredible result. Jim leaves us breathless with his sweeping visions of a landscape sandwiched somewhere between the ether and the smallest grain, while Richard allows us to marvel at the minutiae of the mortal and the everyday – as in the 'twin rusting hulks of oil tanks' of 'Purteen Harbour' and 'concrete spatter scree' of 'Sea Lion'.

Richard and Jim have often said to me that the west is full of contradictions. Like a raging fire on a cold night, it can be tempestuous and sullen... soothing and serene. It's a landscape blessed with a thousand different faces and a thousand ever-changing moods, constant only in its unpredictability. Maybe you've been lucky enough to glimpse gentle shafts of morning light dancing on the waters of Galway Bay or watched the bogs and battered rocks of Roundstone and Errisbeg cower beneath angry clouds. Maybe you have marvelled at the sun slipping down over Rosses Point or witnessed the Atlantic raging against the shores of the Mullet Peninsula. If you have, you'll understand what they both mean... if not, then you will be inspired by this journey.

Ria Higgins
Sunday Times

Introduction

I first met Jim Kavanagh in London at the opening of an exhibition of paintings by the late Denis Bowen, who turned out to be a mutual friend. Denis introduced us and we did not stop talking until the early hours of the following morning. I later met Jim at an opening of his own work in the Crypt Gallery under Saint Martin's in the Field in central London. I was powerfully drawn to what I saw there, Jim's experimental use of materials – mixing oil paint and aerosol car-paint, different chemicals interacting on the canvas, working flat on the floor of the studio and letting the painting take part in its own making.

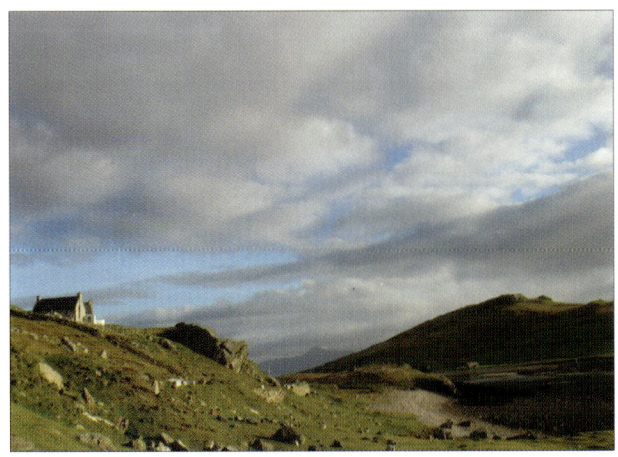

Jim combined a close attention to materials with a deep artistic sensibility and a rich knowledge of the history of art – mostly self-taught. I greatly admired Jim's honesty and directness in an artworld which was becoming increasingly caught up in the cult of the personality and the ethics of the pop industry. But above all I valued his friendship.

I wrote several catalogue essays for Jim's London exhibitions and to my surprise two of them spontaneously transformed themselves into poems ('Solve et Coagula: The Alchemical Opus of Jim Kavanagh' and 'The Poetics of Space'). When Jim and his wife Anne Riordan moved to Galway I started to visit them on a regular basis; it was important to maintain our friendship unimpeded by distance. I was immediately impressed by the extraordinary landscape of the west of Ireland and fascinated by the way in which it had transformed Jim's

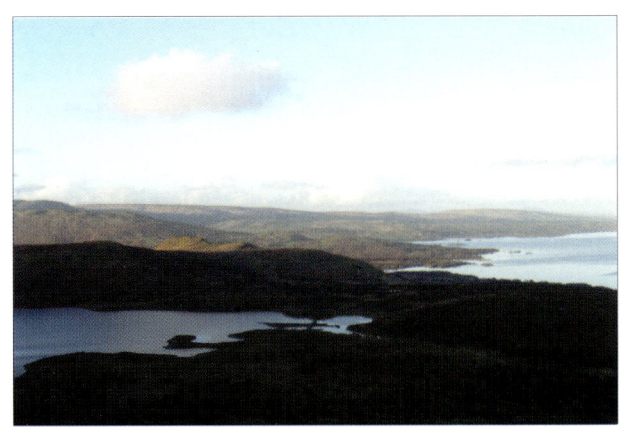

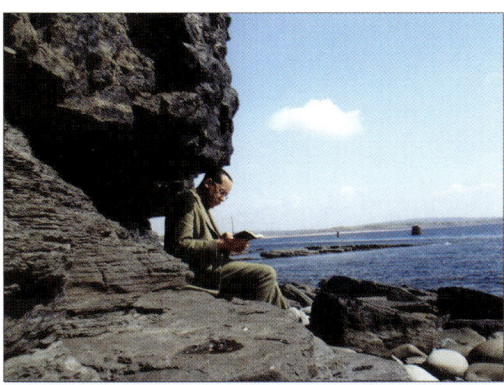

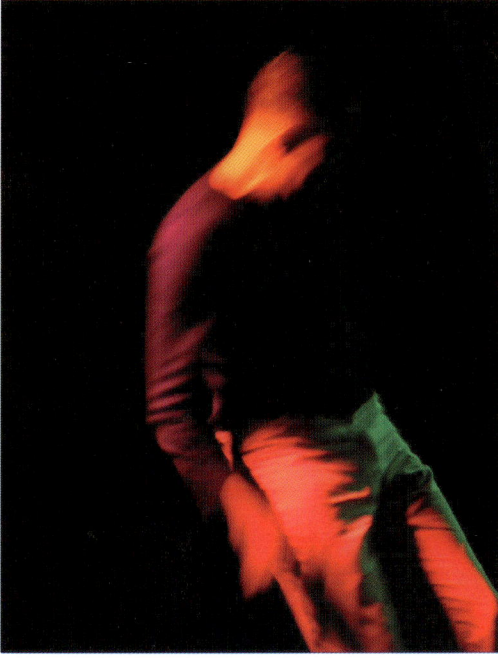

work. It is such a powerful influence on his practice that I do not believe he could ever have made these paintings in London's grey-skyed, car-fumed gloom. We began to develop the idea for this book over several visits; both mine to Galway and Jim's to London.

The importance of collaboration was central to the project. Jim's paintings were not going to be 'illustrations' to my poems and my poems were not going to be 'descriptions' of Jim's work. Over several months we retraced Jim's 'Western Journey' and I responded to the same places that had inspired him – only this time through the medium of poetry. From Annaghdown we ventured out to the extraordinary terrain of The Burren, the overwhelming vistas of the Maumturk mountains, the dizzying hights of the Cliffs of Moher and the serene seascape of Bertra Beach. Sometimes we would only travel as far as Lough Corrib, just behind the house and studio in Annaghdown, at other times as far as Achill Island and the Aran Islands. All the time I wrote in my 'little black book', one I had not used for years, but in which I realised I had made the first drafts for some of my most successful poems. It was like a good luck charm, and it seemed to work very well.

Sometimes the poems are very much about the place, a direct response to the geography of a particular location, such as the 'The Cliffs of Moher' and 'The Burren', at others the poetry is more to do with my state of mind at the time of the visit, mediated through my emotional resonance with the location, for example, 'Suspension;

Annaghdown (Cuildermot Woods)' and 'I Looked Down'. At others an unexpected incident was the impetus for the poem, as in 'Sea Lion: Purteen Harbour', where we stumbled across the extraordinary and moving sight of a huge Sea Lion's carcass mummifying on the shore.

I have endeavoured to open myself to the phenomenal landscape which is the west of Ireland in the same way as Jim has so successfully done in his paintings, I hope in some measure I have succeeded. Jim Kavanagh is undoubtedly one of the most important painters working in the west of Ireland today and it is my great hope that this book will bring his work to the attention of many new admirers.

Richard Dyer

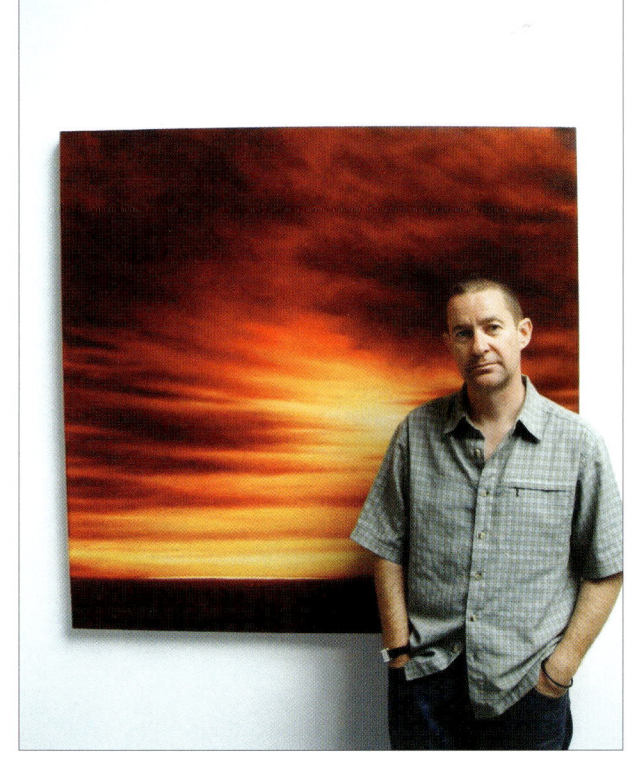

The Journey

Cladach Cuín
oil on canvas
170 x 80cm

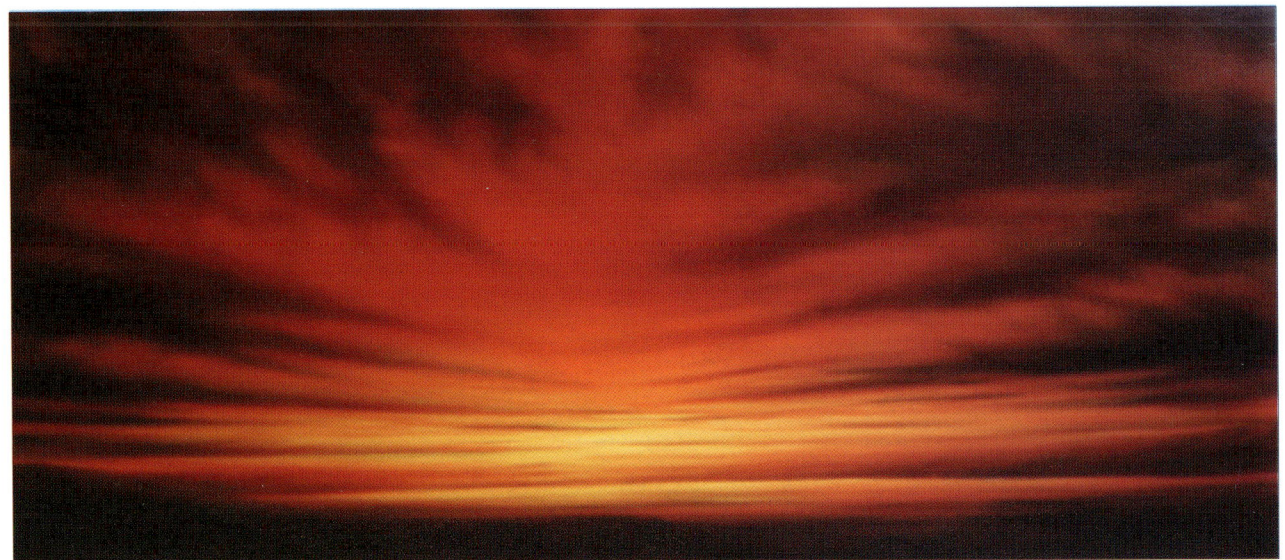

Connemara Mountains
oil on board
61 x 41cm

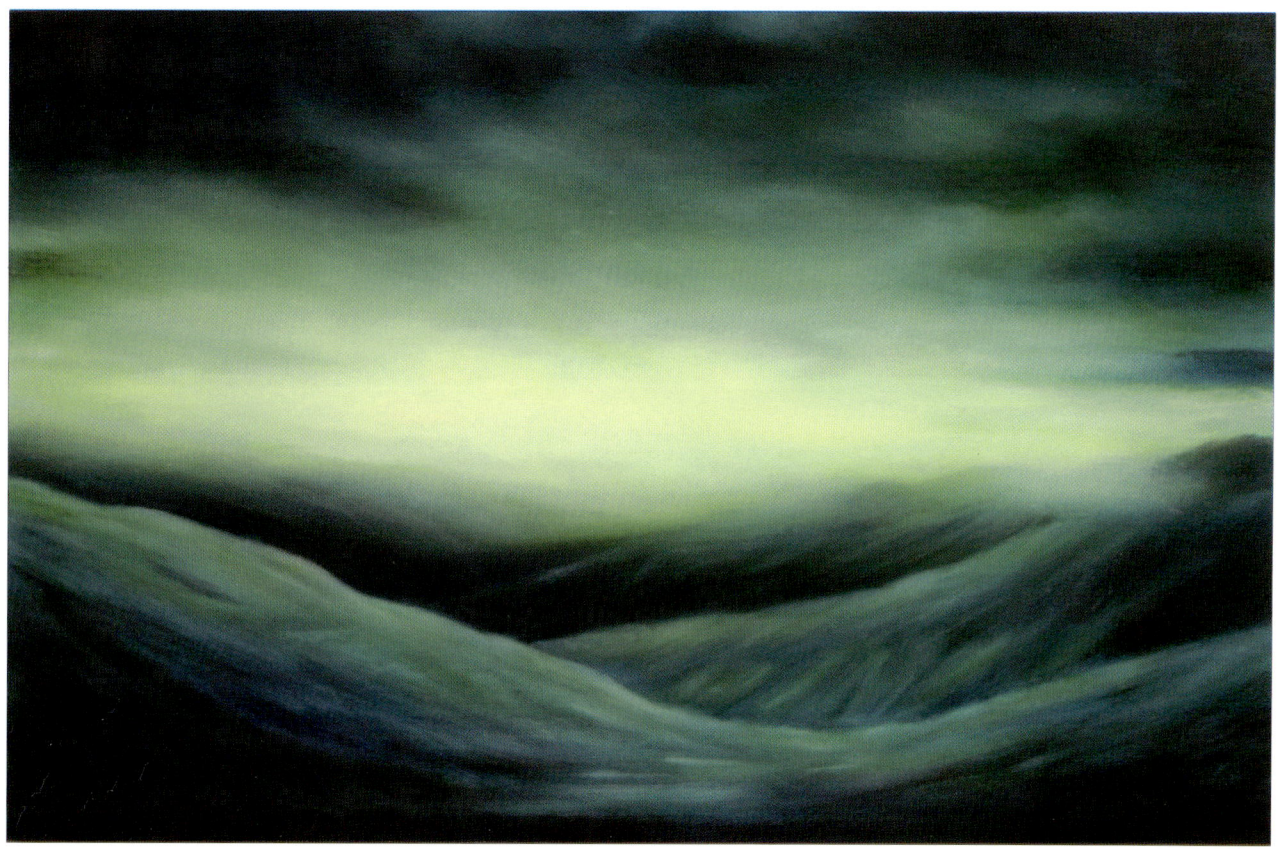

The Cliffs of Moher

Over the crest of the road
I see the sea, leaching
Into the grey haze of the day.

We walk past the up-turned
Rib cage of a bitumen covered
Currach, trapping light like a black hole.

A polychrome cacophony
Of polythene net-floats sun-
Bleached buoys and rotting netting

Leading to a limestone beach
Of wave-shaped granite boulders
Here in light-filled Liscannor Bay.

Spring-soaked rock shelves
Green clad with moss algae
Hint at Cliffs of Moher.

A gothic cathedral of
Rusty Easter Island statues
Staring out to sea.

The molecular sparkle of
Sun photons on sea crests
Flips into digital dance-light,

Suddenly the air is crowded
With an agitated cloud
Of antimatter horse flies

Trying to match trajectories
With the salt sea light-swarm, but
Missing the trick of stitching time.

Wild grass waves breaking over
The top of drystone walls, indigenous
Igneous rock, crumbling in slow-time.

The Cliffs
oil on board
41 x 41cm

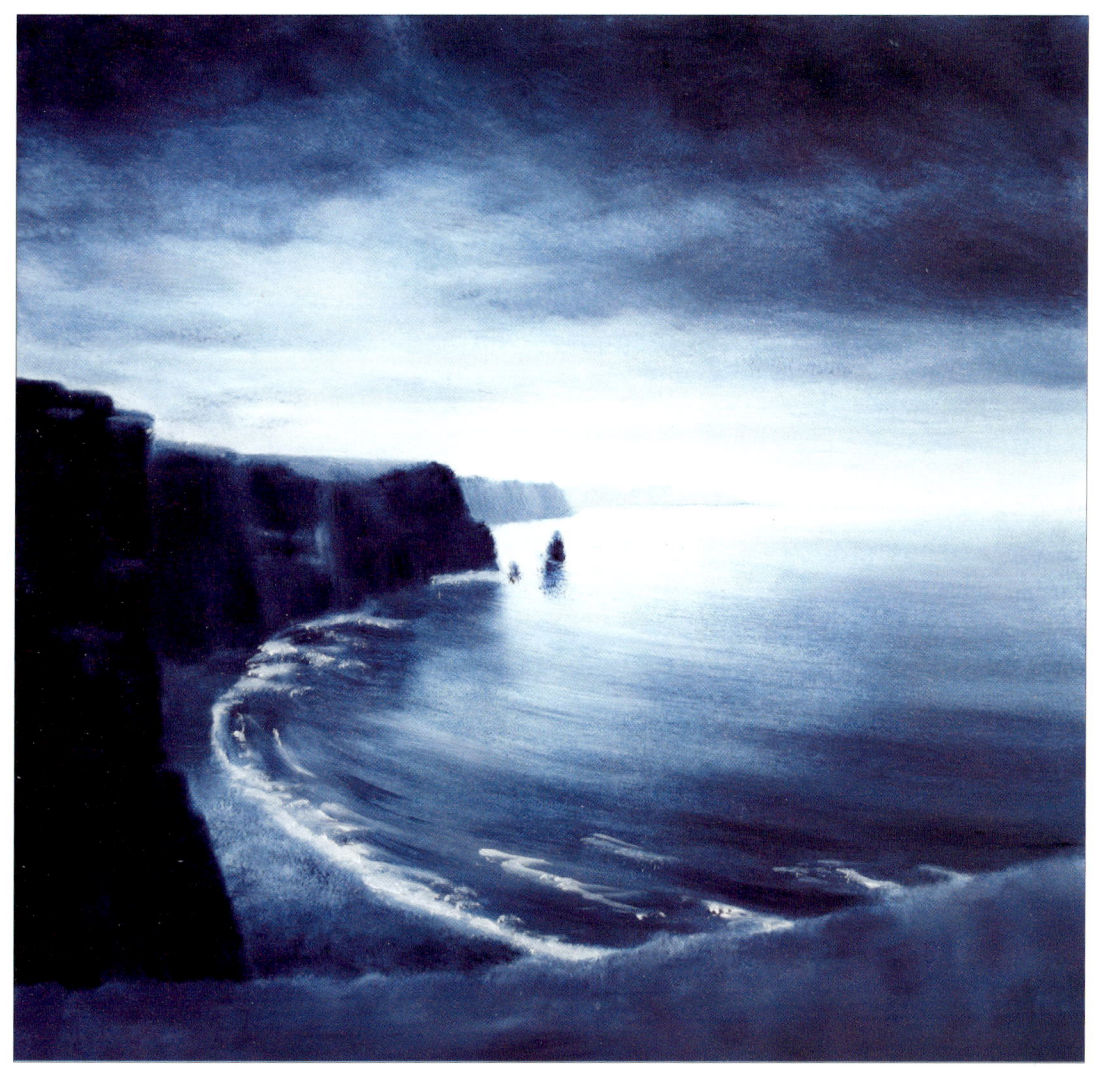

On Bertra Beach

On Bertra beach I feel the pressure of Croagh Patrick
heavy on my back, I sense the weight of rock against
my spine, I look out to the cold Atlantic sea, but know
that I will have to turn, the hills have eyes and they are
burning in my back. The grey-green peak is resting
mossy fingers on my shoulder, urging me to turn
and meet its gaze. I feel the pressure building, like the
lump rising in my throat when I knew the next stop on the
tube was yours, our last. The Atlantic leaks into my eyes
and Bertra Beach becomes a blur. At last I turn towards
Croagh Patrick in a daze. It fills my eyes to the edges
with its bulk, Leviathan but somehow weightless in the air,
it is as if it is not there at all, but painted on the inside
of my eyes. And now I stand with Bertra Beach behind me
Patrick's peak drawing me to its summit. I feel the ache
within my limbs already, although I have not taken one step
up the mountainside. In my dream that night I glide up the
sloping reek like a kestrel on the crest of a moonlit cloud.

Light Over Croagh Patrick
oil on board
91 x 61cm

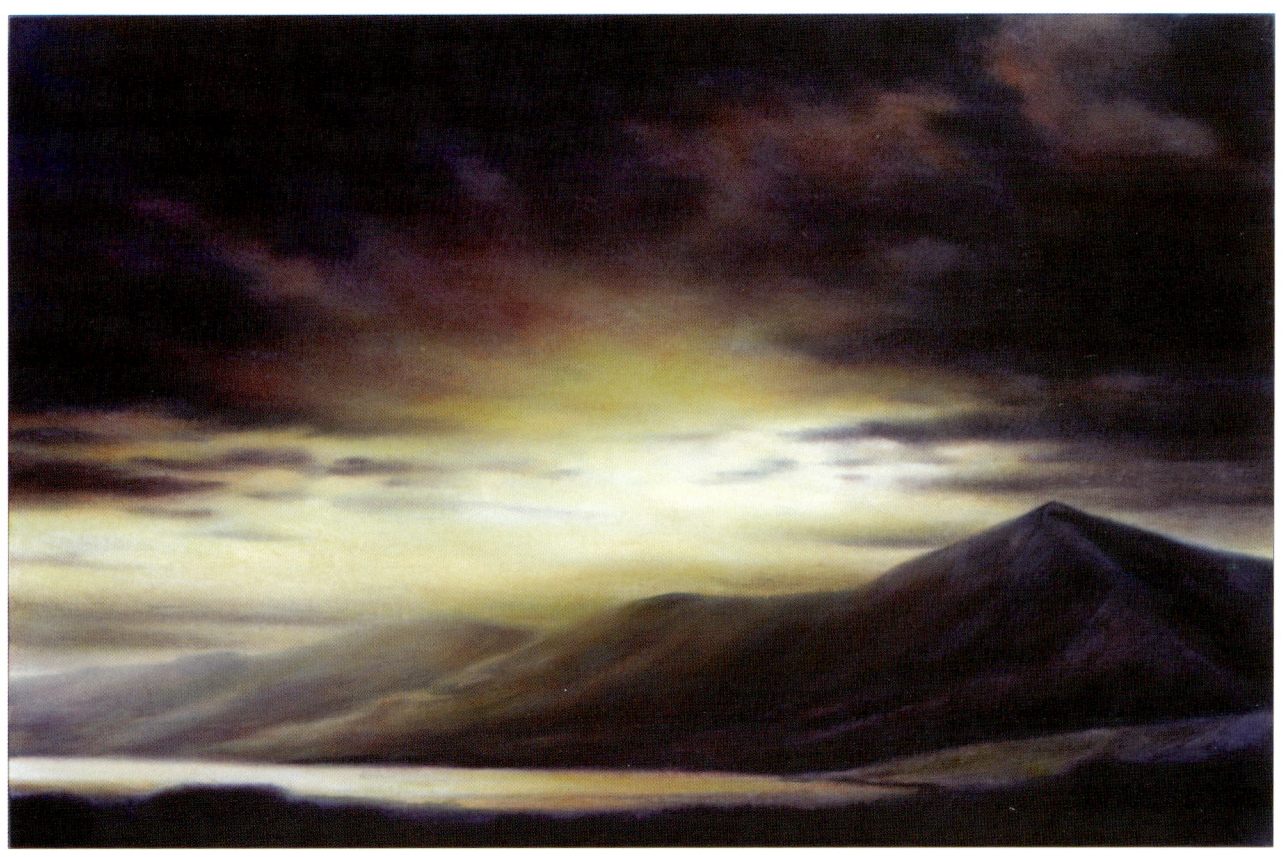

Mount Gable

The hollow ghosts of houses
shrouded in a milk of mist,
limestone walls, solid as centuries,
guard the vacant space of passed
lives long departed, private
histories seeping into
soft damp stone dark soil.

Where once stone floors declared
this space as man and woman's
home house place, nature now
lays her soft carpet of moss
and lichen there. Fire grates which
once burnt turf now grow it back,
whatever mark we once made
on this land is now reclaimed.

Trunks of trees now occupy
the space where table legs were
once so firmly planted on the
stone, branches bud in place of
chairs, hawthorn bushes spikily
reclaim the space of former
beds, larks hop on ironing boards
and book shelves, squirrels bury
acorns under the floor-boards.

Tall towers of rain rise up
vast pillars of a watery
cathedral, making the vision
of the abandoned houses of
Gorr Riabhach shimmer in and
out of focus, as if they were a
mirage, as if at any moment they
might disappear into the damp air.

Mount Gable
oil on board
91 x 61cm

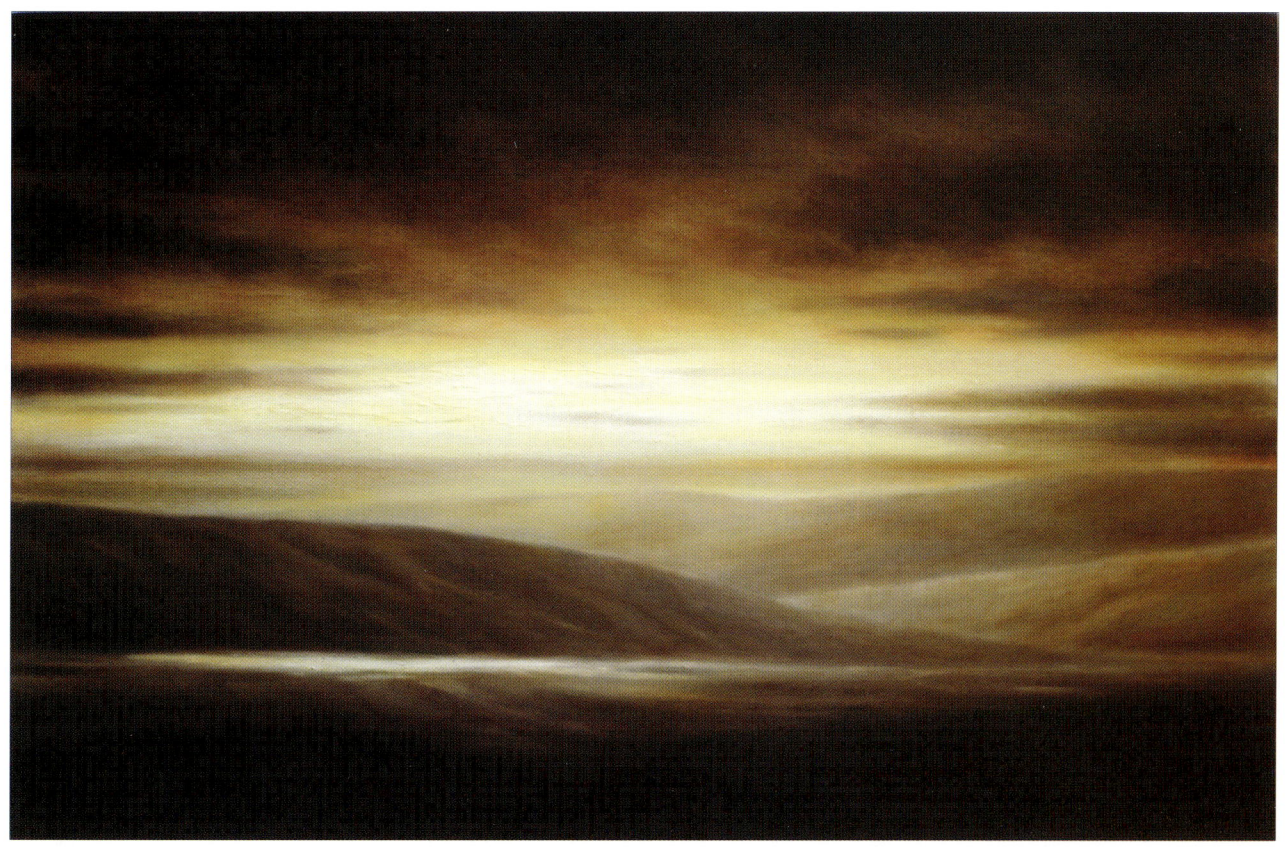

Devil's Mother
oil on board
61 x 41cm

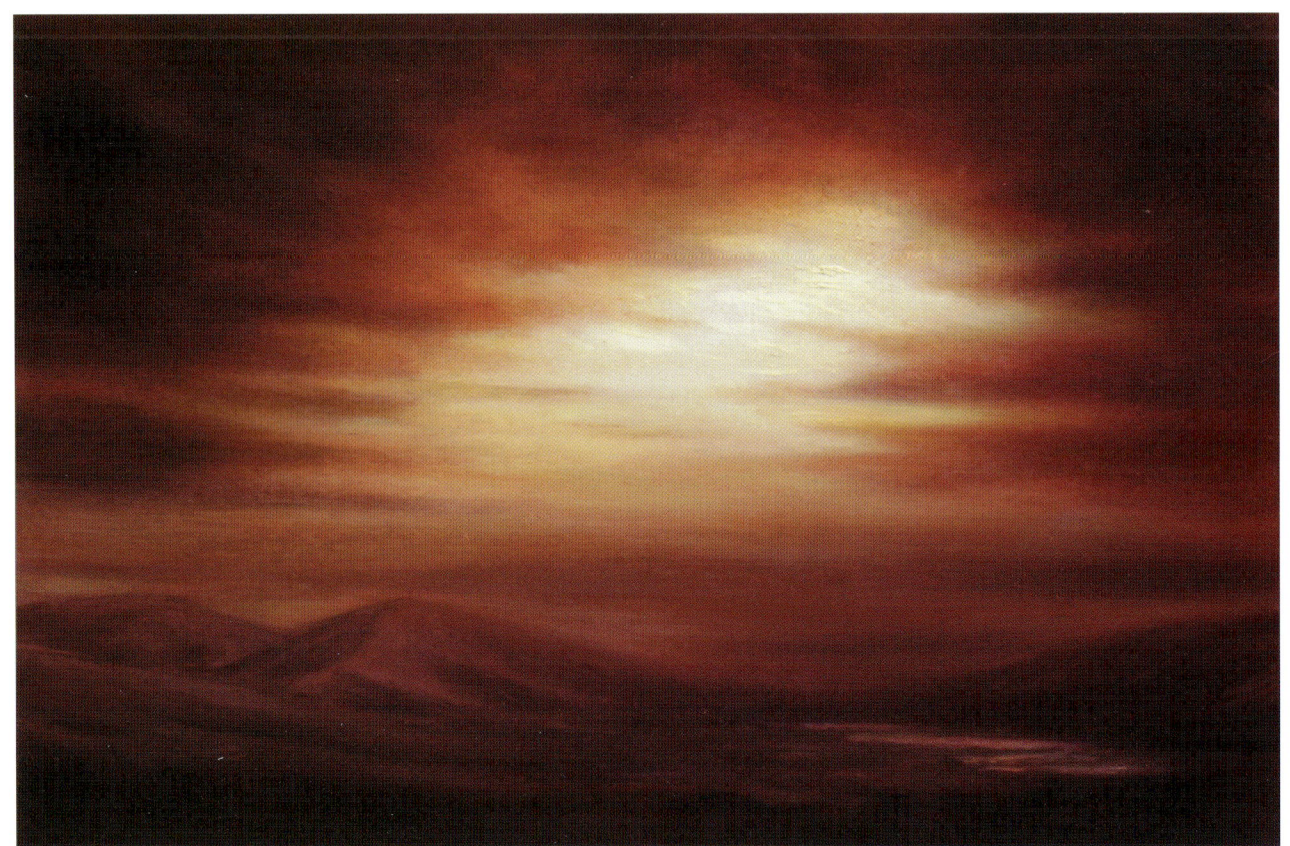

The Maumturks
oil on board
102 x 56cm

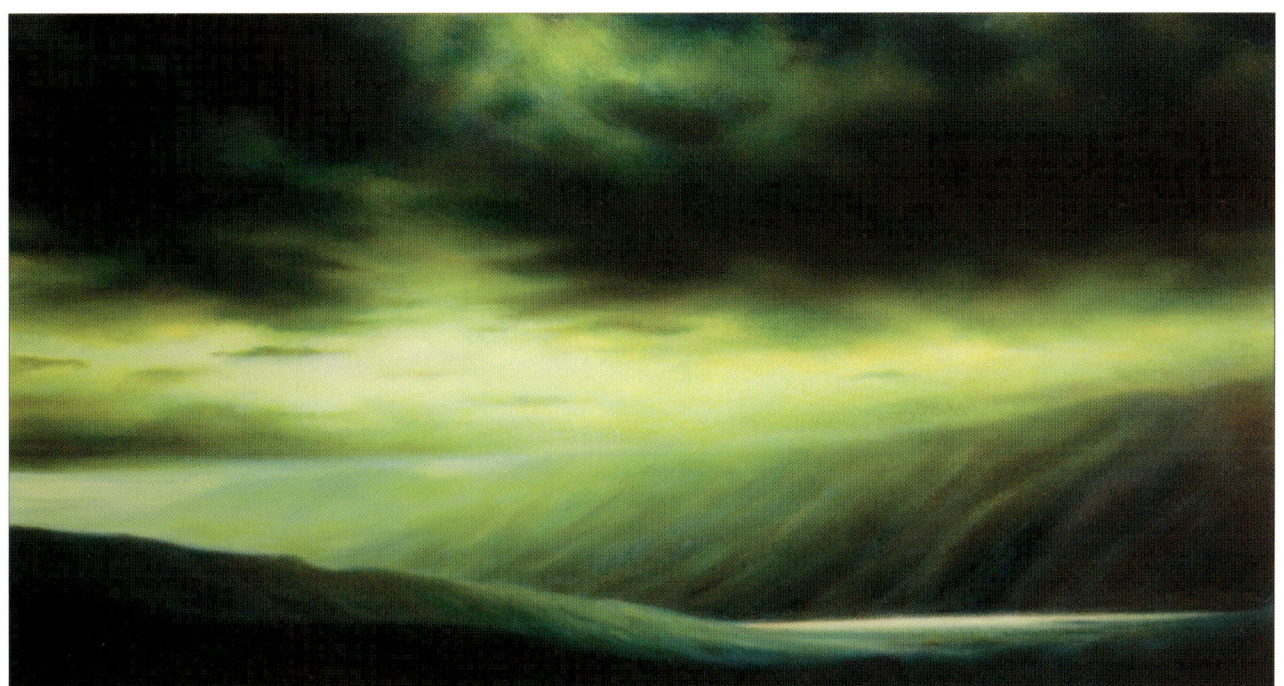

Killary Harbour

Motoring around Mweelrea mountains
We slide the car into Killary harbour
And slip into Gaynor's welcoming warmth
To watch a game of Gaelic football;

Basketball, rugby and soccer, all
Rolled into one. The chill dark pillars
Rest on the bar beside us, almost untouched
Creamy sandstone slabs afloat on

Cool obsidian cylinders. A flock of baseball
Caps above the bar. The window is full of
Mountain, the room is full of Guinness
Soft and creamy as silk, dark and cold as coal.

In the stone wall a perfect square of fire, in
The window a perfect square of stone; Ben Gorm.
After many minutes I realise I have been listening
To Gaelic – not English; I have understood it all.

We head for home, cloud shadows on the Sheefry
Hills, along the Doo Lough Pass, the setting sun
Catching on the lacerations of the famine scars
I drift to sleep, thinking of the millions gone.

Leenane Mist
oil on board
76 x 51cm

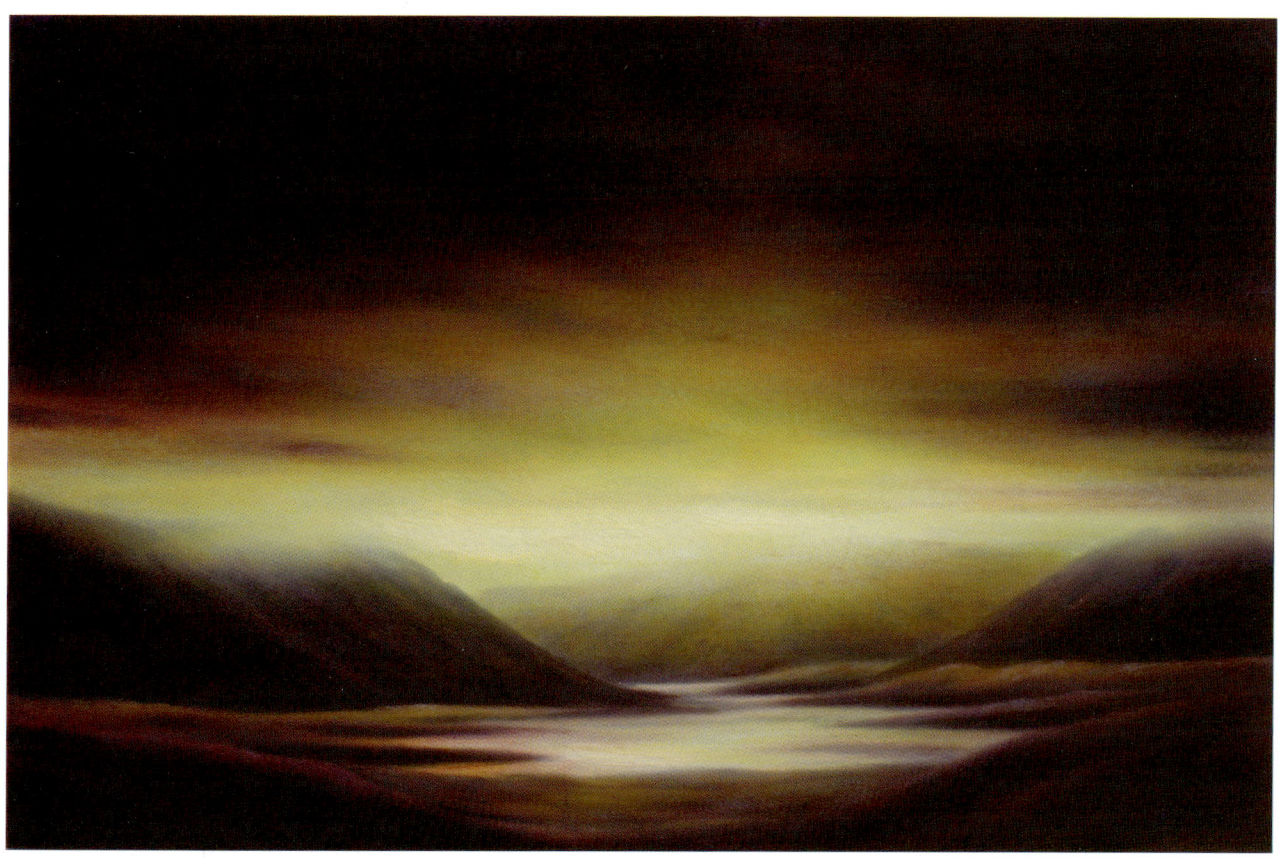

Longing For
oil on board
71 x 56cm

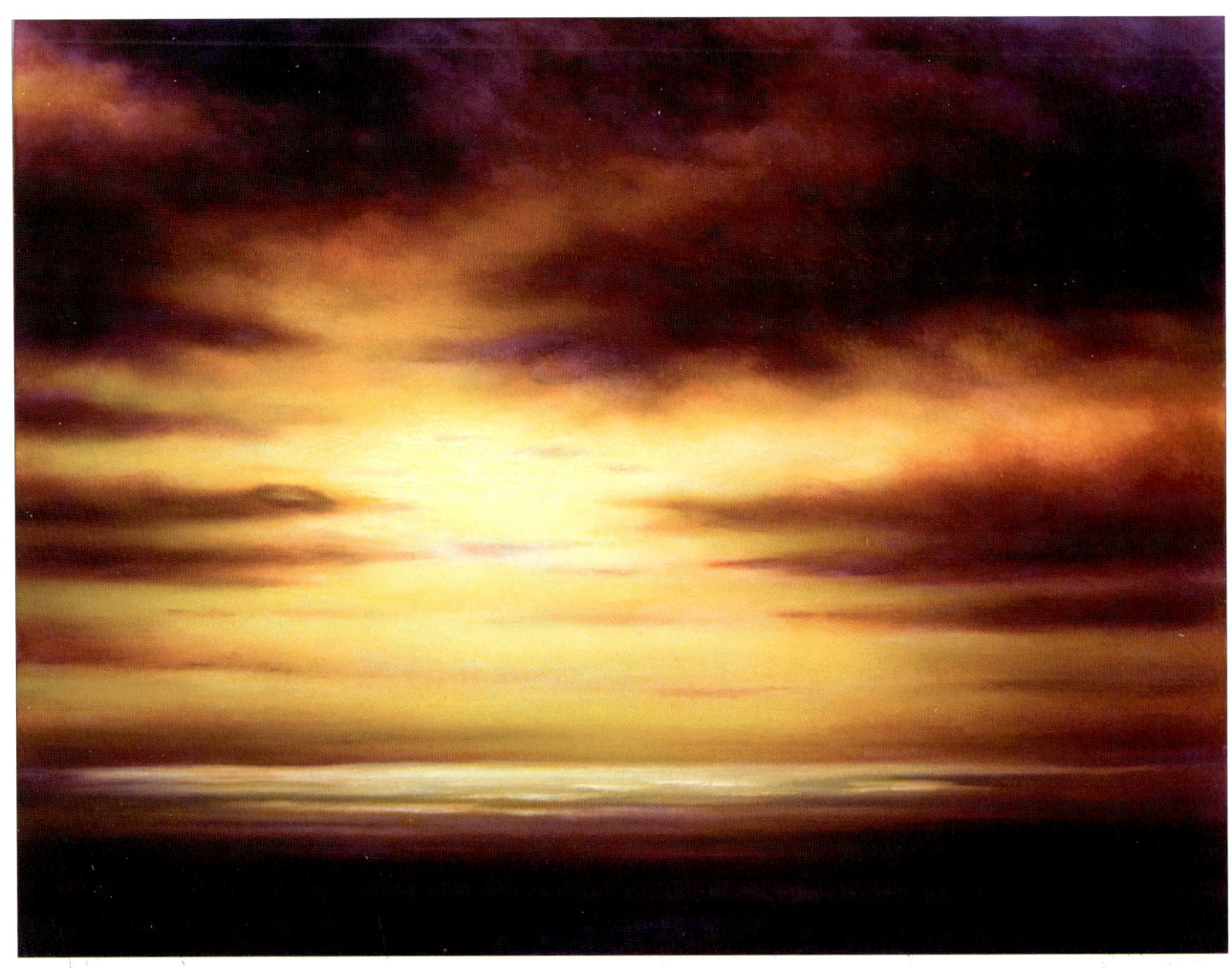

Suspension
Annaghdown (Cuildermot Woods)

Your body suspended
In the humming blue heat,
Spherical particles
Of sunlight illuminating
Your luminous skin, water
Droplets rising in three-
Dimensional space to
Meet your glorious beauty.

The whole vision, a liquid
Stereoscope of desire.
I hold it in my eyes,
Walk around your floating
Loveliness, parallaxing
Your body with the moss
Green trees behind; for a
Moment you are mine forever.

It is as if time has stopped.
A bird hangs in the air
Above you, wings spread,
Spanning the solid space
In mid-flight, its feathers
A filigree of perfection.
I know it cannot last.
I blink, and it is gone.

Galway Bay
oil on canvas
122 x 61cm

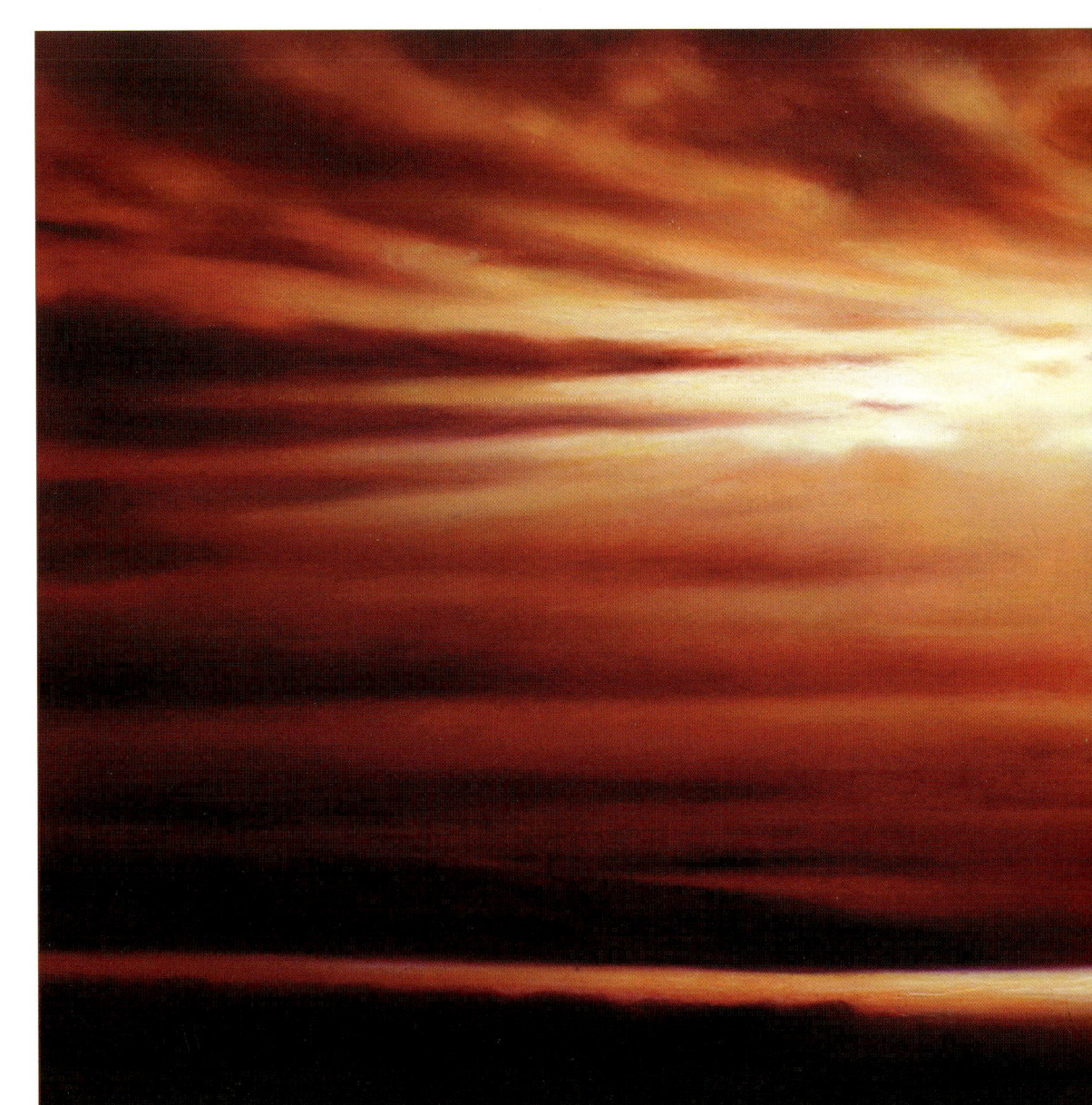

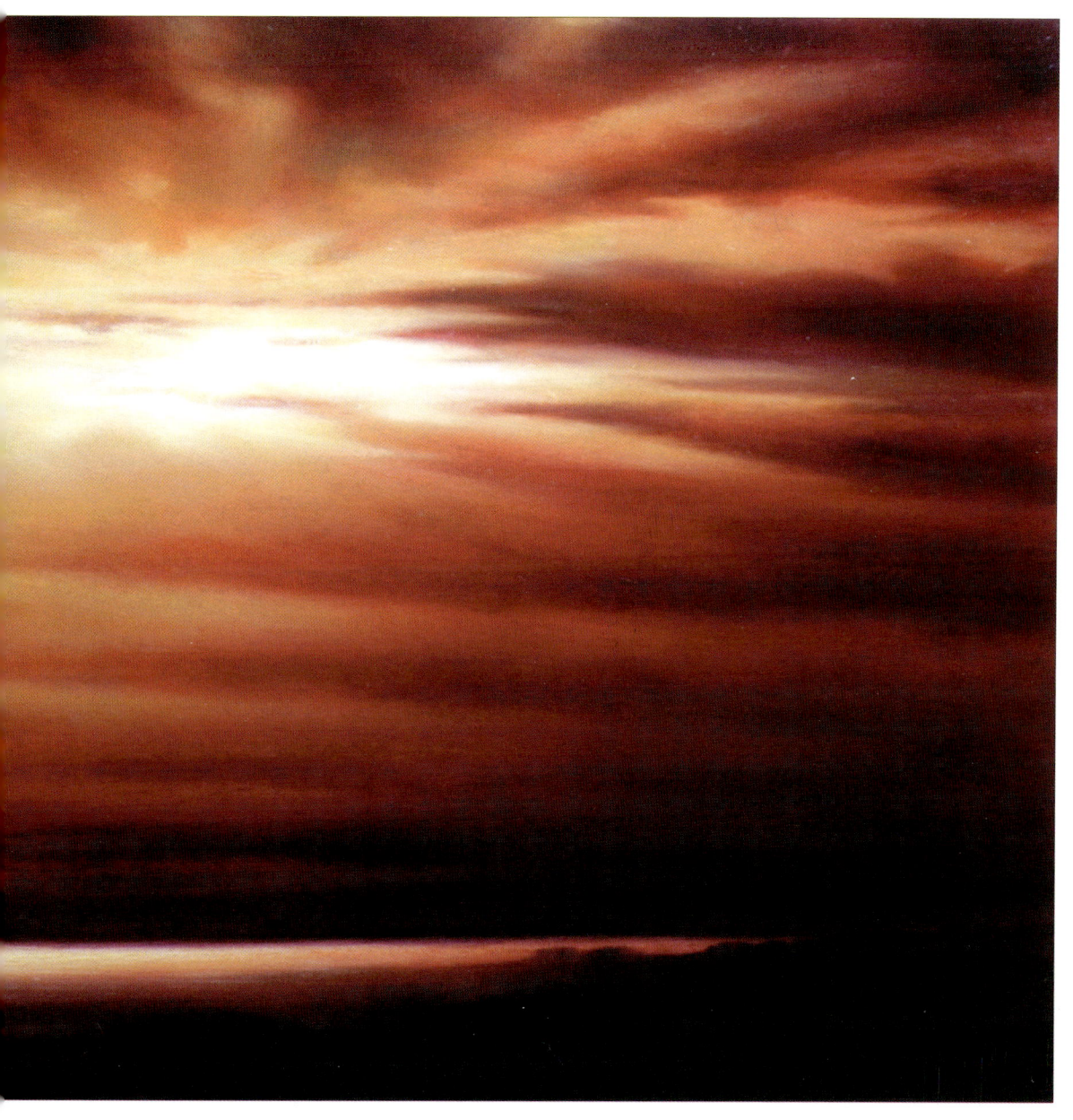

Purteen Harbour

PURTEEN WT.140, D808 WT143,
SIGI II, WT 192, REALT NA,
THE HILDA, MARA, WALRUS.

The harbour boats wait for the
sundown's blush, rock-weighted
lobster pots, nylon green rope

tangled with red string, fresh sea
stench filling my headspace
FORD 3000 tractor, rusting,

hunched by the harbour's edge,
old dog tied to a chain, hump-
backed boats hiding in the green

hollows of the turf-sea, keel spines
bleaching in the sun-scorch,
sheep whittling the grass verge.

SILVERSEA tyre-propped
on the quayside, the twin rusting
hulks of giant oil tanks

soak in the last rays of the
sun, rivets stitching them
into the harbour-space.

Sea Lion
Purteen harbour

Amongst the broken rockscape
I see the slick-rot of a sea lion's hulk
Almost the size of a full-grown man
Carcass drying in the last rays of sundown
Skull screaming for its final meltdown
Ribs curling through its slowly melting
Shrinking thick skin, alien skull
Drying in the sun-spoil, rusty oil cans and
Plastic bleach bottles its final funerary
Ornaments, penis-bone lurching one last
Time through the desiccated dry skin.
Sunburnt flipper-feet strangely crossed now
As if he is relaxing; this is where we all go.
And on the quayside the broken
Husk of a boat prow, memorialised
With concrete spatter scree, rust nails
Sticking up from its broken rib-cage
Now a ram's retreat from the harsh wind.

Dark Light
oil on board
91 x 61cm

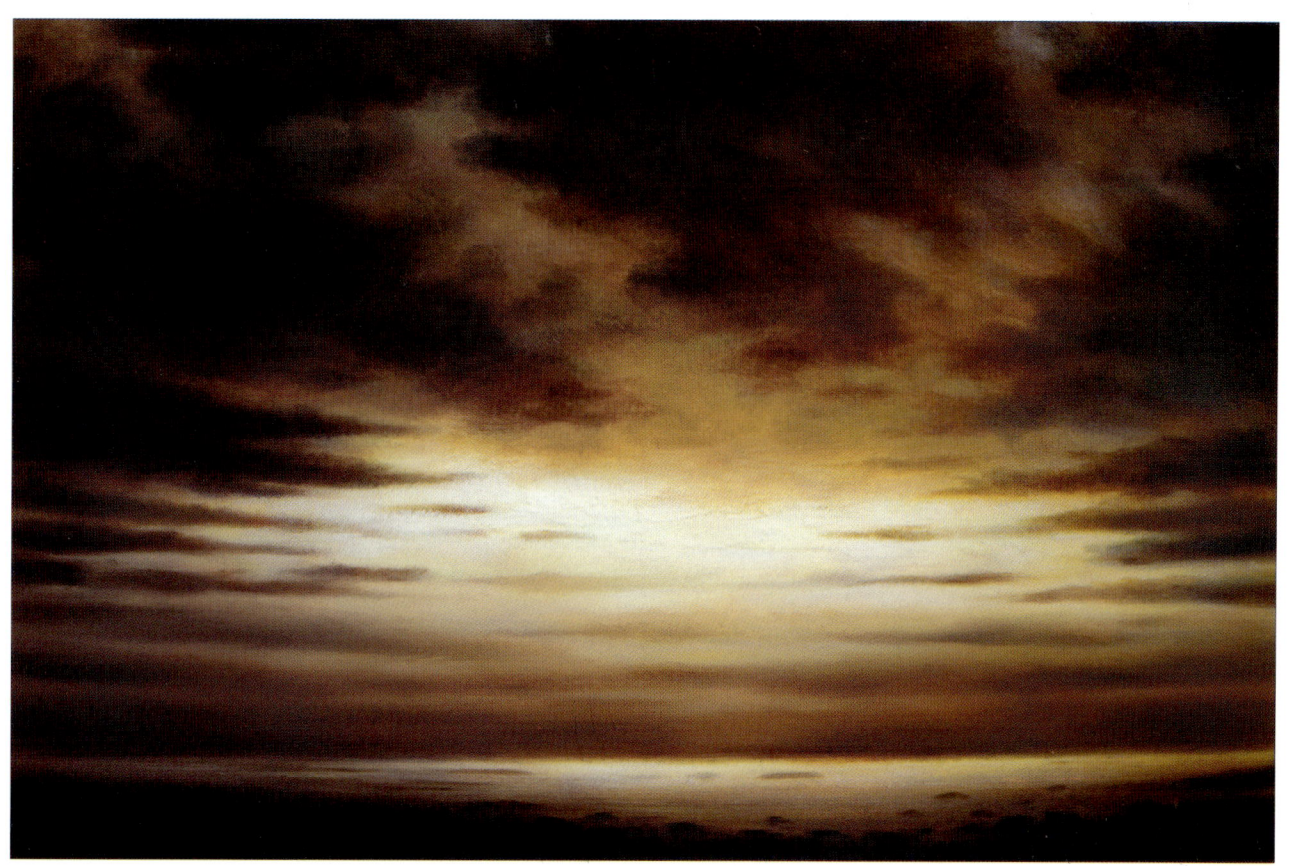

Keel at Dusk
oil on board
122 x 61cm

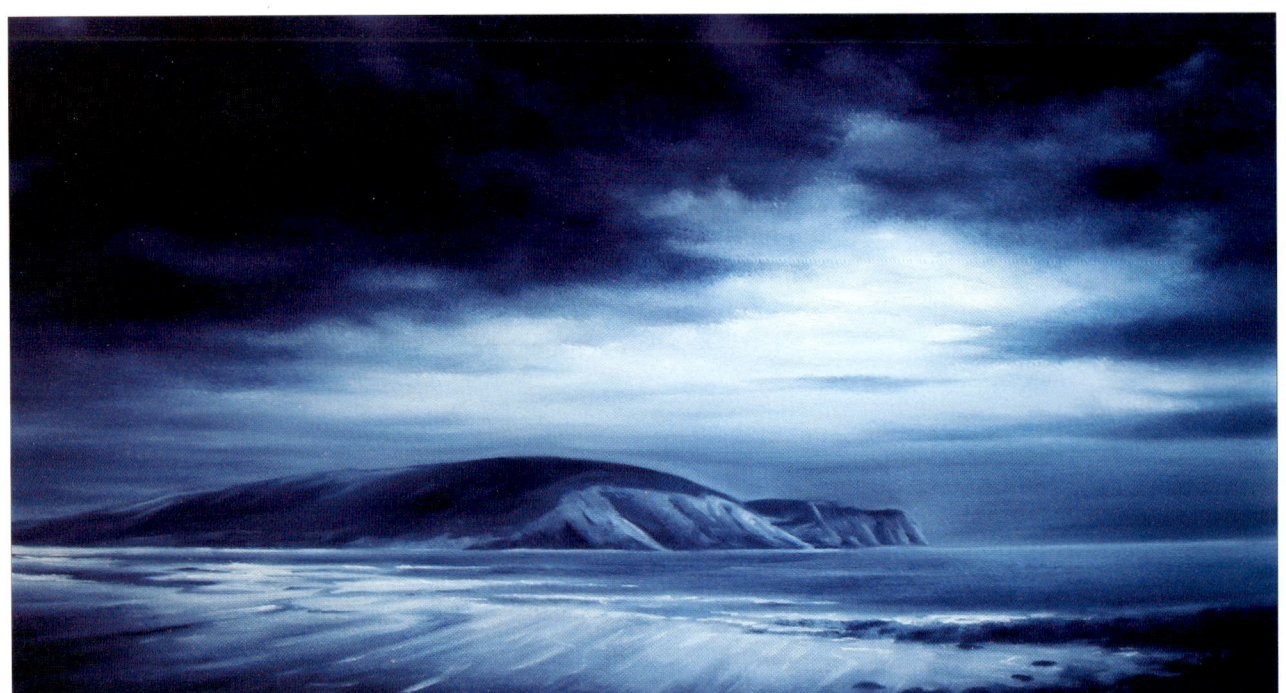

Keel Beach
Minaun Mountains

The sky is rolling down the
hill a giant hand of cloud.
Bounded by the crab-backed
green-clad hill on my right
sun-drenched Minaun Mountains
left. Keel beach spells out
bereft, in a Morse-code of
amber pebbles, a brail-trail
of footprints and seaweed.

The empty eyes of the house
stare out to sea, beneath the hill
the soft cotton of the sky is falling
to the Earth. We drive up the
mountain road and gently collide
with a cloud, it wraps its chill around
the car. Suddenly there is a glass-still
man-made lake, a valley reservoir
clouds hugging the stone scarred hills.

He Sizes Citadels of Light
Curragh Line

At night the sky eats
The white meat of the moon.
The wall of weeping willow leaves
Nods back and forth, back and forth
Engaged in endless conversation
With the waves that slowly choke
The thin white neck of sand
That stands between this window
And the dark green tunnel
Of the moonlit clad and
Over-salted sea, which
Seizes citadels of light and
Throws them high into a
Waiting sky to make a
Milky Way whose beauty sticks
In our throats like marble dust.

Citadel of Light
oil on boad
61 x 41cm

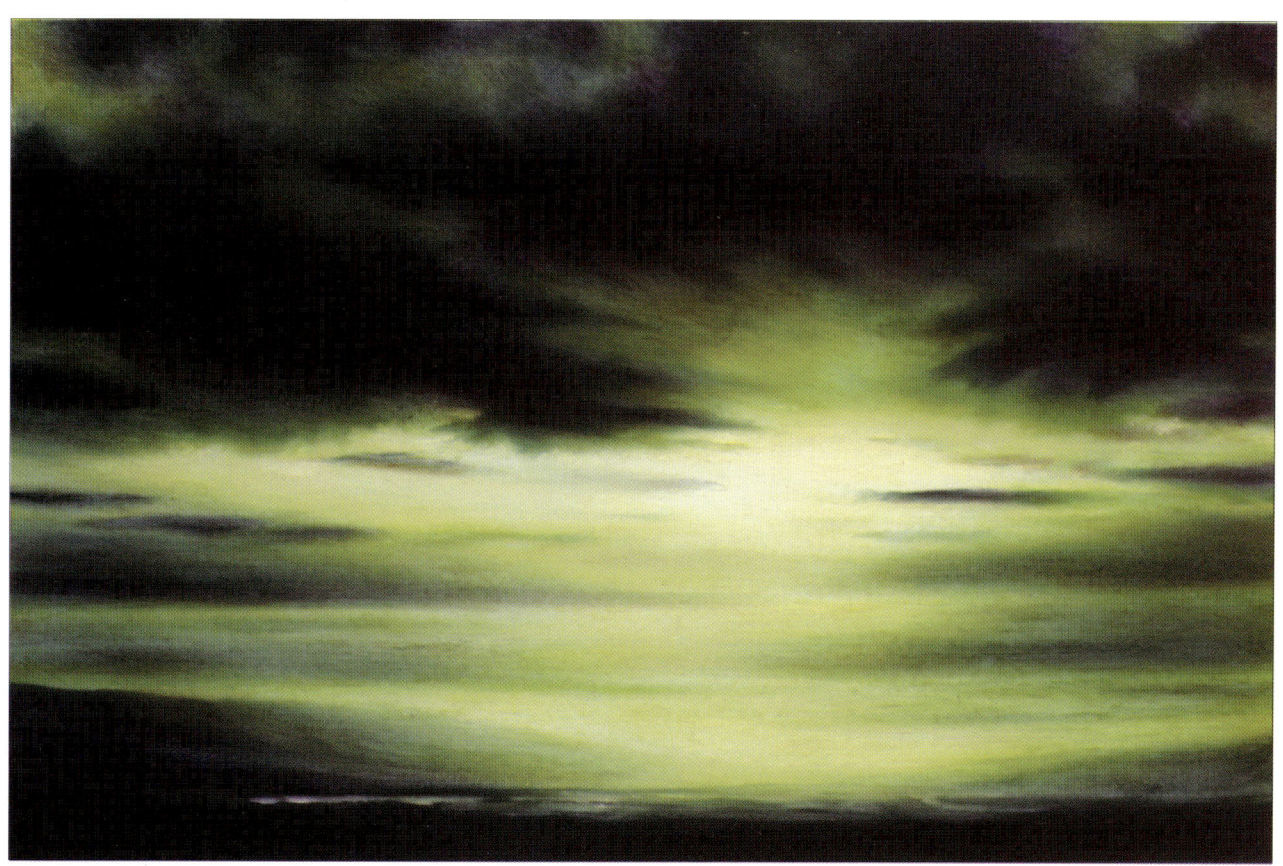

Achill Island

On the road to Castlebar
my eyes are full of signs
Partry Road, Ballinrobe,

Castlebar. The sleeping
Elephant of the hill, Tonragee,
lays its trunk down to the sea,

its soft green weight hugs the
strata deep below. Passed Breks
Stone to the bridge to Achill Isle.

The grey pudding of the
mountain is steaming with
rain clouds, its dark form

haunting the horizon. Down
Atlantic Drive, Cursa na Farraige,
roadside rams graze the grass bank.

Passing over the bridge to
Achill Isle I feel a sense of floating,
as if we have stepped aboard a boat.

The island is a hollow hulk moored
loosely to the blue-green sea, at any
moment it might float away.

Atlantic Eve
oil on board
40 x 40cm

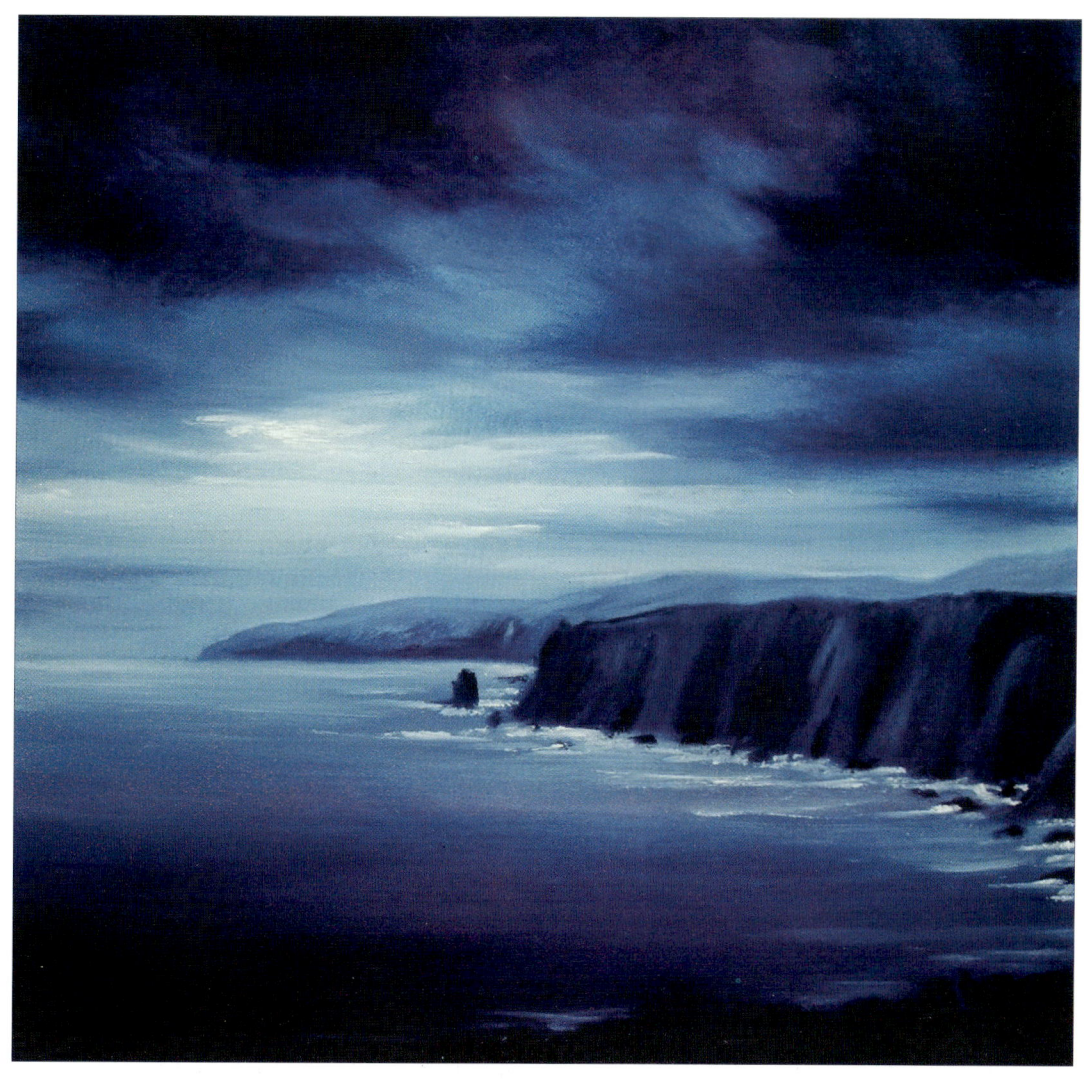

Clew Bay
oil on board
122 x 46cm

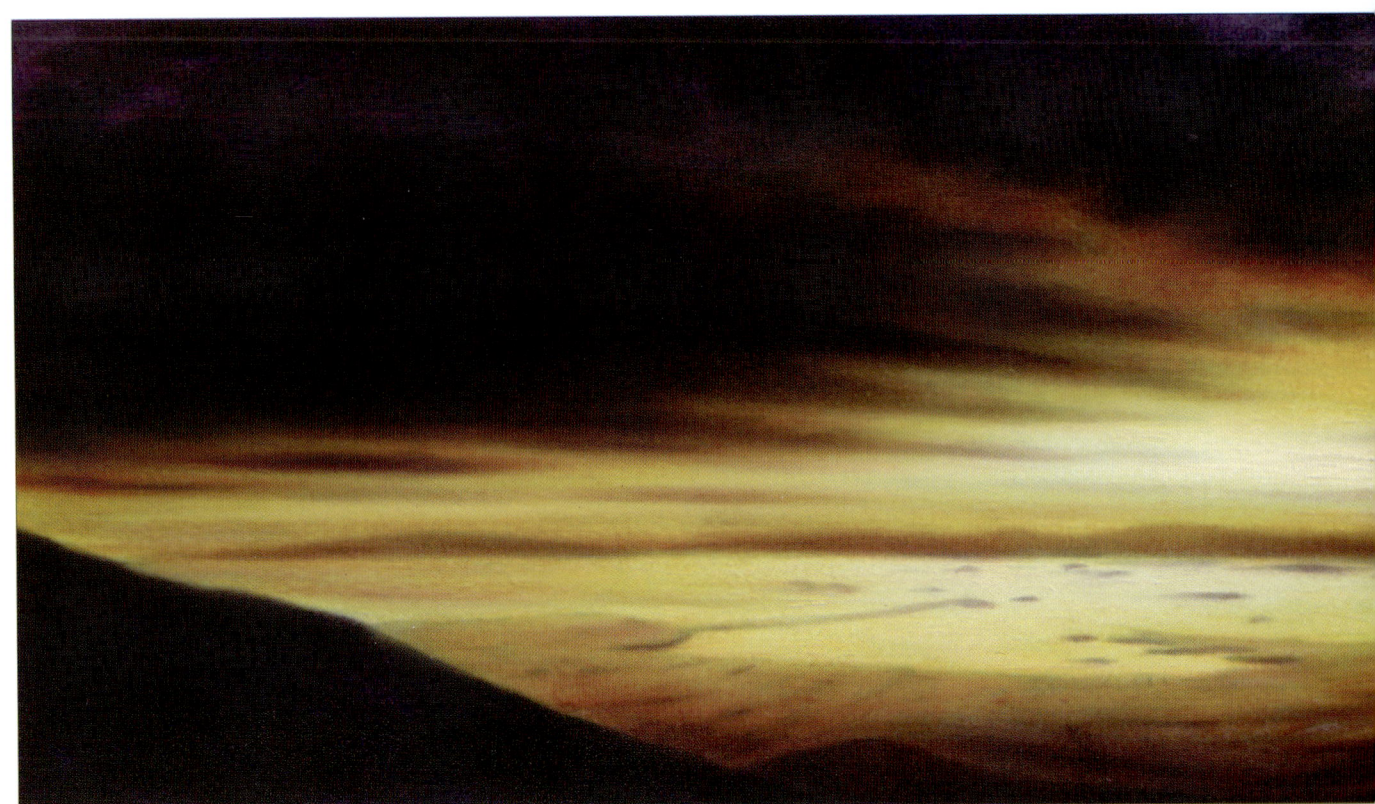

I Looked Down

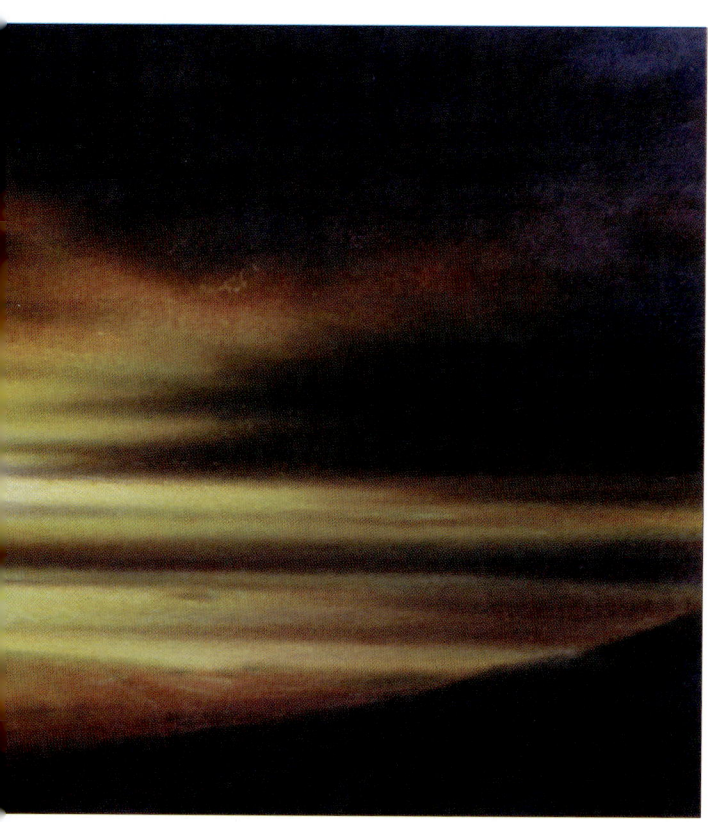

I looked down to where you sat
beneath the cliff and saw
two grey black shards of rock
break loose above your head
and fall towards you but before
I could shout out my warning
they opened wide slate wings
and slipped silently into the sky
above your head as you looked up
startled by their sudden shadows
and turned to smile at me pointing
at the life-mated pair of herons
as my heart beat hard in my throat.

The Day's Reflection
oil on canvas
127 x 78cm

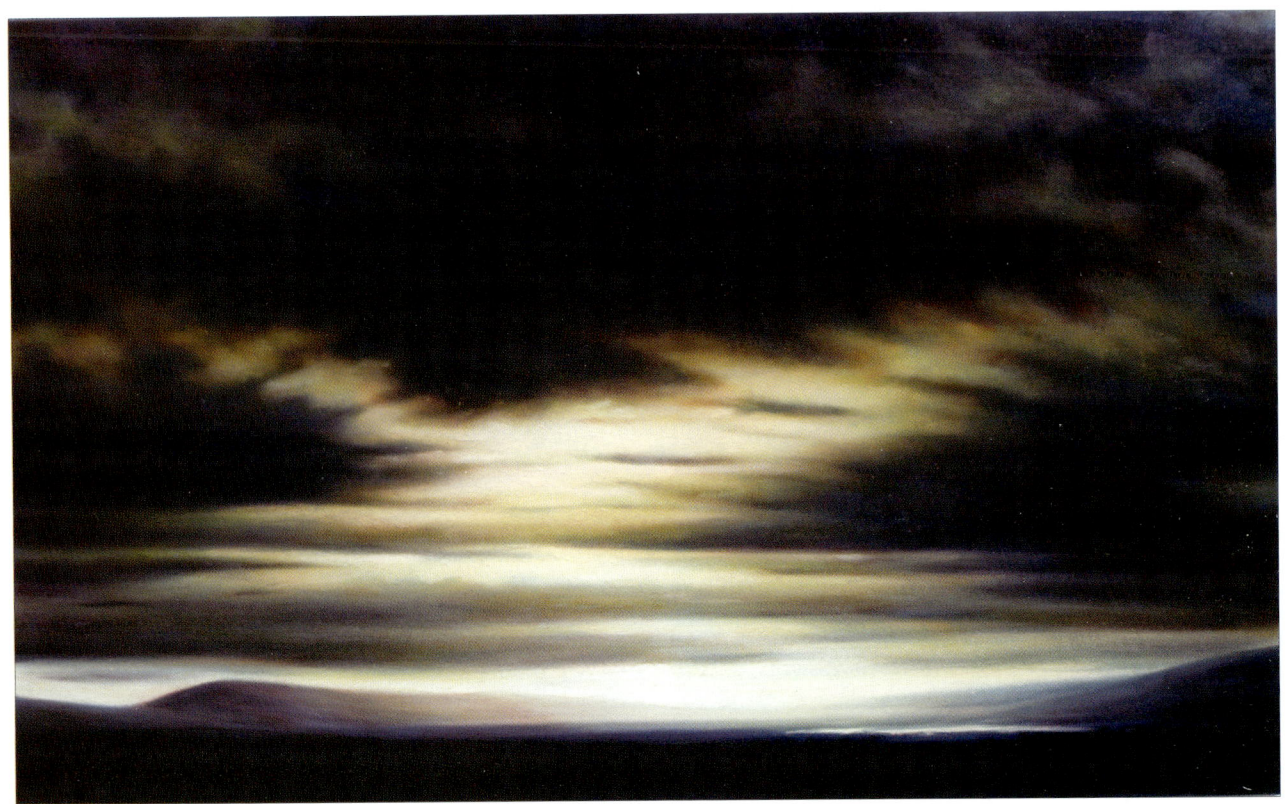

The Poetics of Space

The plush velvet of a purple sky at dusk,
the crush of clouds against the edge of darkness
at the dawn; the sun's blush, a comet's streak against
the vacuum of the night, the rush of light, the glaze,
the harvest of the night. An inner sense of indigo,
invisible in red, the canvas, a fabric cauldron
for the colours of the curdled clouds, a bed.

A sense of place, a sense of moment, melting,
spent, the incremental reconfiguration rent
by sudden shifts of mist; the surging of the elements,
a fist, gripped tight and pulled to twist the canopy
of fragile molecules into a memory of the earth beneath,
the country in the sky; mirage, illusion, shadow-play and lie.

Horizon's crease folds sky to landscape down, a Rorschach stain,
a sacred wound, bound black and flecked in sun-down's golden crown.

The canvas lays flat on the studio floor, a gout of honeyed light
aches through space to lace it with a tracery of
Venice turpentine, stand oil and siccative; into this
liquid territory a violet underpainting firms and
structures space. Later layers of transparent colour cool
and warm the raw imprimatura to fix a final vision
of the landscape – Croagh Patrick, Connemara – and
the deserts of Arizona, Utah and Nevada.

Cloonacauneen Castle
Guinness

There is a single second
When the pint settles,
Suddenly it turns from
Brown swirl to black ink,
In an instant; as dark
As interstellar space.

I stroke the mist from
The side of the glass
To test the cast from
Brown to black, to see
If the foaming haze has
Settled into a dark infinity.

But still the amber bubbles
Rise like liquid geologies.
Then it is ready for me.
It is like drinking the skin
Of snow from the crest of
The Maumturk mountains.

It tastes like burnt ash, like
Star-dust, like blood from a bitten
Lip, like lead paint chewed on window
Frames and varnish on chair backs
Back then, coal dust, your sex, ear
Wax wet, our second kiss when

We wept, when we bit hard,
Mingled blood foam, roamed
Around each other's inside space
Moaned, bit again. If this is life,
Then I like it very much, and it is
Life Jim, but not as they know it.

Galway Town

The time it takes for a pint of
Guinness to set is the speed of a
Cloud across the sky of Annaghdown.

I am hung over, I am strung out,
down the teaming high street, of Galway
Town, busy as a stream of leaping

salmon, when I realise everyone
I pass is in the same state as I,
eyes as glazed as plates, tongues

hiding in the dark chamber of last nights
long late fun, breath best kept in lungs
and safe from this exchange.

Into the thankful darkness of
the Front Door Pub, for a transforming
transfusion of the dark sacrament.

Stout stands in for wine and bread
replaced by haddock chowder, creamy
and warming as a hug from a friend.

And moon-globe lights alight
above young Tom, they usher
night-time into day. We hide until

We must head home, third turning
down to Annaghdown, exactly twelve
and one half miles from Galway town.

Finny, Mayo
oil on board
71 x 56cm

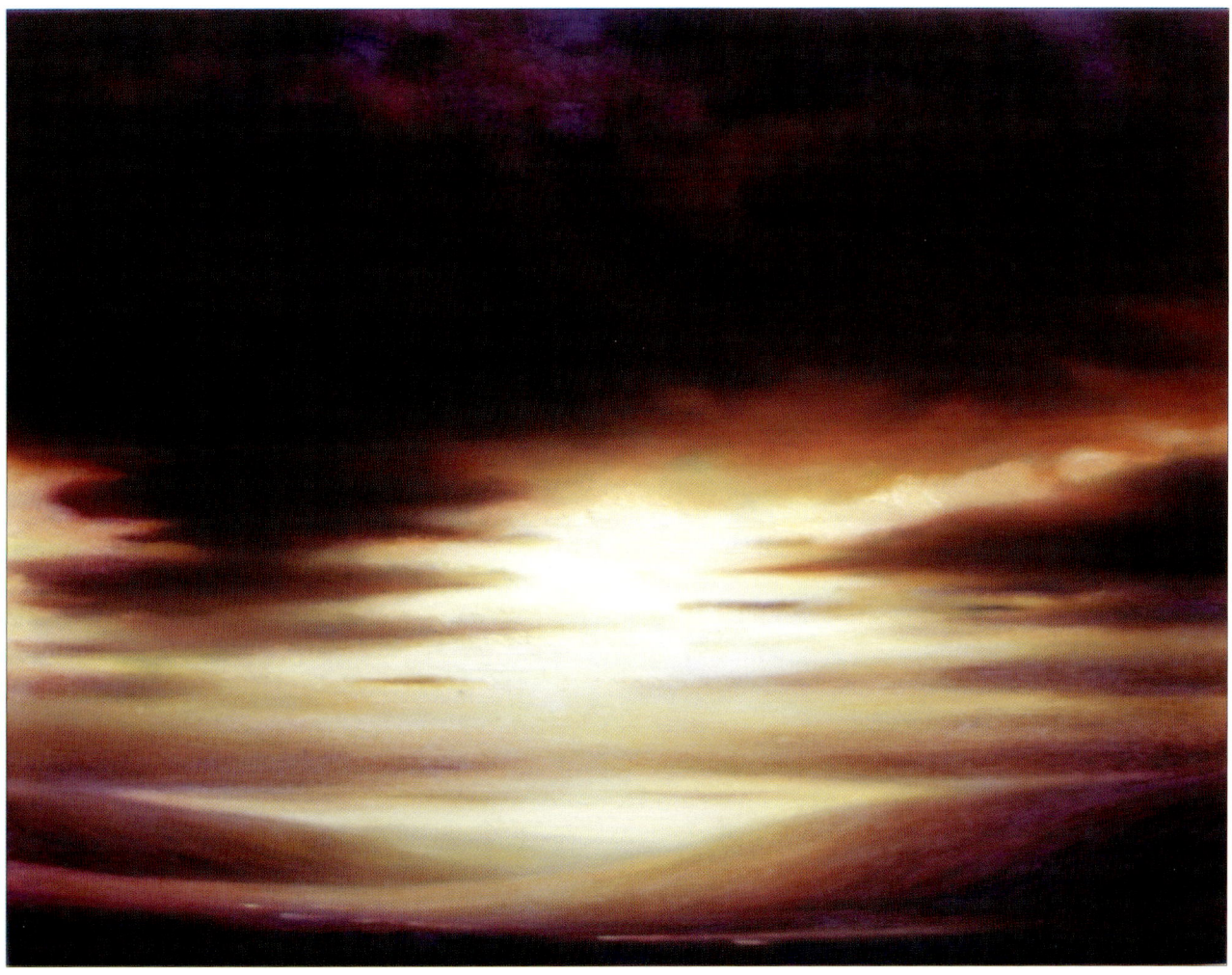

The Burren

In County Clare, where all the trees lean east
and drystone wall-gaps let the wind breath through
we drive from Ennis up to Corrofin and on to
Lisdoonvarna. In the Burren upland now, we look
down onto Galway Bay, the scent of thyme catching
the day in memory's net. Heart's tongue, common violet,
blue gentian, herb robert scatter colour through the bare
pavement of the rocks. In Poulnabrone, the hollow of
the millstone, limestone sediment folded and buckled three-
hundred and forty million years ago to form a resting place
for the Portal Tomb. We slide on the rocks, making a sound
like fragments spalling from enamel pots, it is like walking
on an ashen honeycomb. Two tall portal stones, topped by
the capstone cairn rest quietly against the greyness of the sky.
Thirty-three are buried here, babies, children, adults in 3000BC.
Silent in their eathy beds, with stone beads, bone pendants
and flint arrow-heads. Underneath the grikes and clints
of the karst flow subterranean rivers, like veins and arteries,
nourishing the fertile rock, the limestone skeleton of the
Burren's curved whale back hump. In their winterage
the feral goats chew back the hazel scrub, allowing
all this beauty to breath in spring and summer months.

From the Burren
oil on board
122 x 61cm

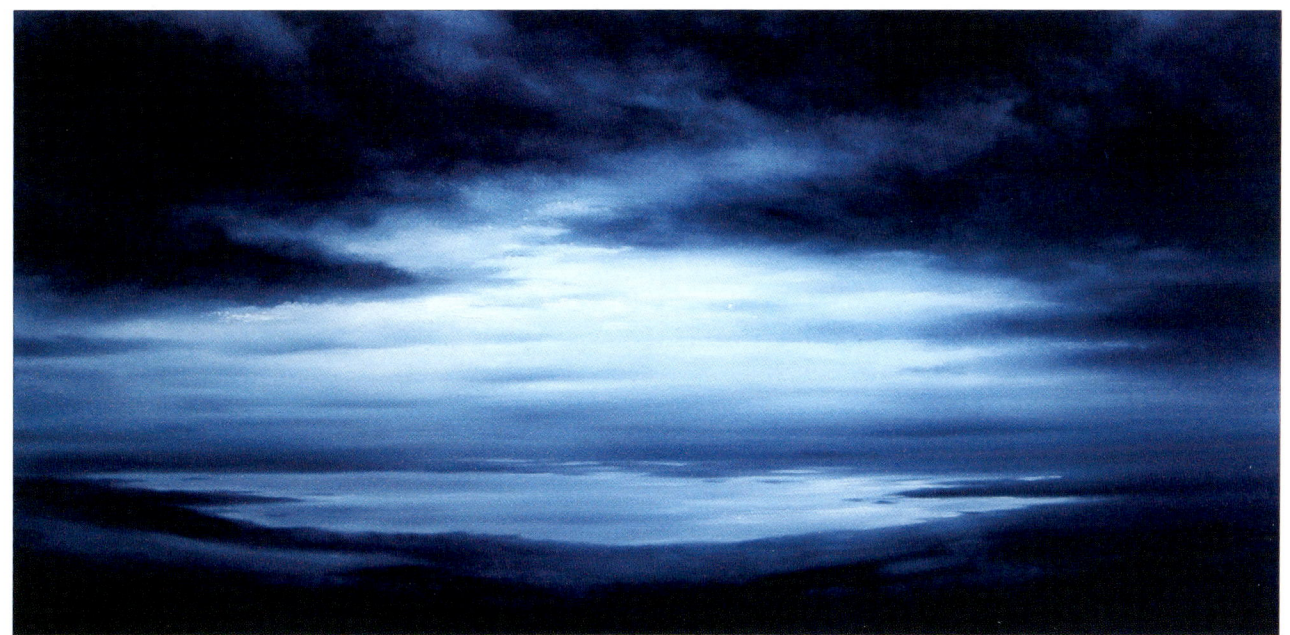

Keem Strand

I wait for the words to arrive
they wash up one by one
an orange beach ball bleached
to the flesh of a peach, blue
nets creeping slowly up the
rock chip beach. A giant
tanker out to sea turns out to be
Clare Island, surging through
the waves. That rock cleft
lion-pointed out to sea reverses
the angle of the slumbering
cliff face, counter-weights
the isle behind. Dark rocks
float to the surface of the sea
and seem to hover there. The
sunlight satins the planished
pewter of the sea-skin, the
grey dog disappears into a
grey rock, its pink tongue
the only thing I see now.
The clouds kiss the sweet
brim of the hill, whispering
sky secrets into its grey-green ear.

Light on the Edge
oil on board
92 x 46cm (dyptich)

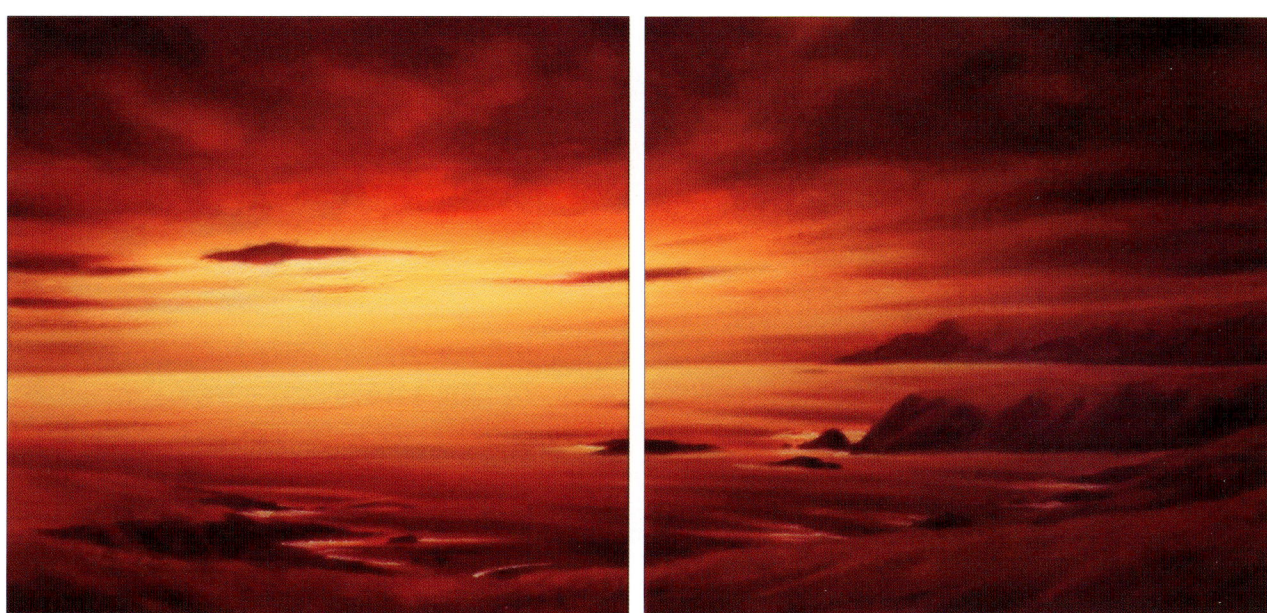

Green Mist
oil on board
123 x 41cm (tryptich)

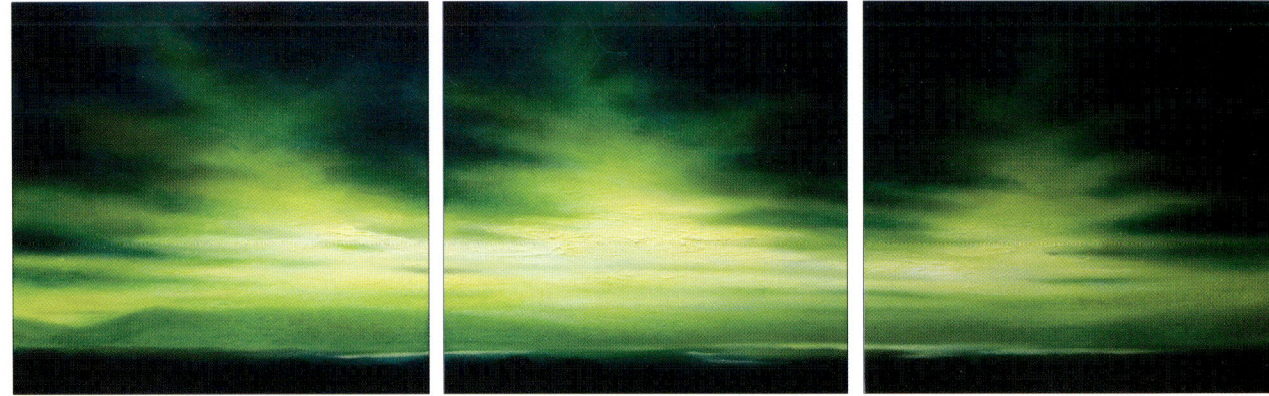

View of the Corrib
oil on board
123 x 41cm (tryptich)

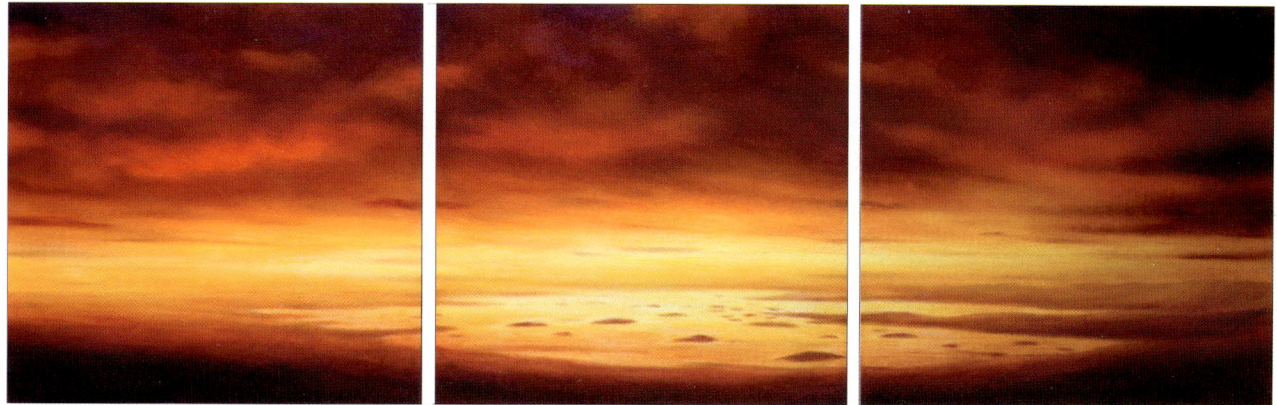

Lough Corrib

Here lies low land slanting,
standing on the slow brim
of the lake: dog, boat, sky,
grass, rock, stone, turf, wind
churning the signature of the
sky, etched in water's vortex eye.

There is a light here, there is
dusk down here, in the home of
the golden ray, deep and dark in
Curved Ballindiff Bay. I breathe in space,
the punctum of the place is laced
inside my heart, I twist and kiss my
words, my art. Purple rock slow
disappearing, land, lake locked
light and shifting sand are nearing.

The Lough shore rim is a sentence
that spells: 'tree, tree, trees, field,
mountain, rocks, wall, church, trees,
reeds, houses, rock.' We always seem
to be in the centre, no matter how far
out we go. The roil of waves around the
boat, the water boiling up behind Jim's
back as the propeller churns the lake
into a pearly dolphin tail of froth.

The Corrib
oil on board
61 x 61cm

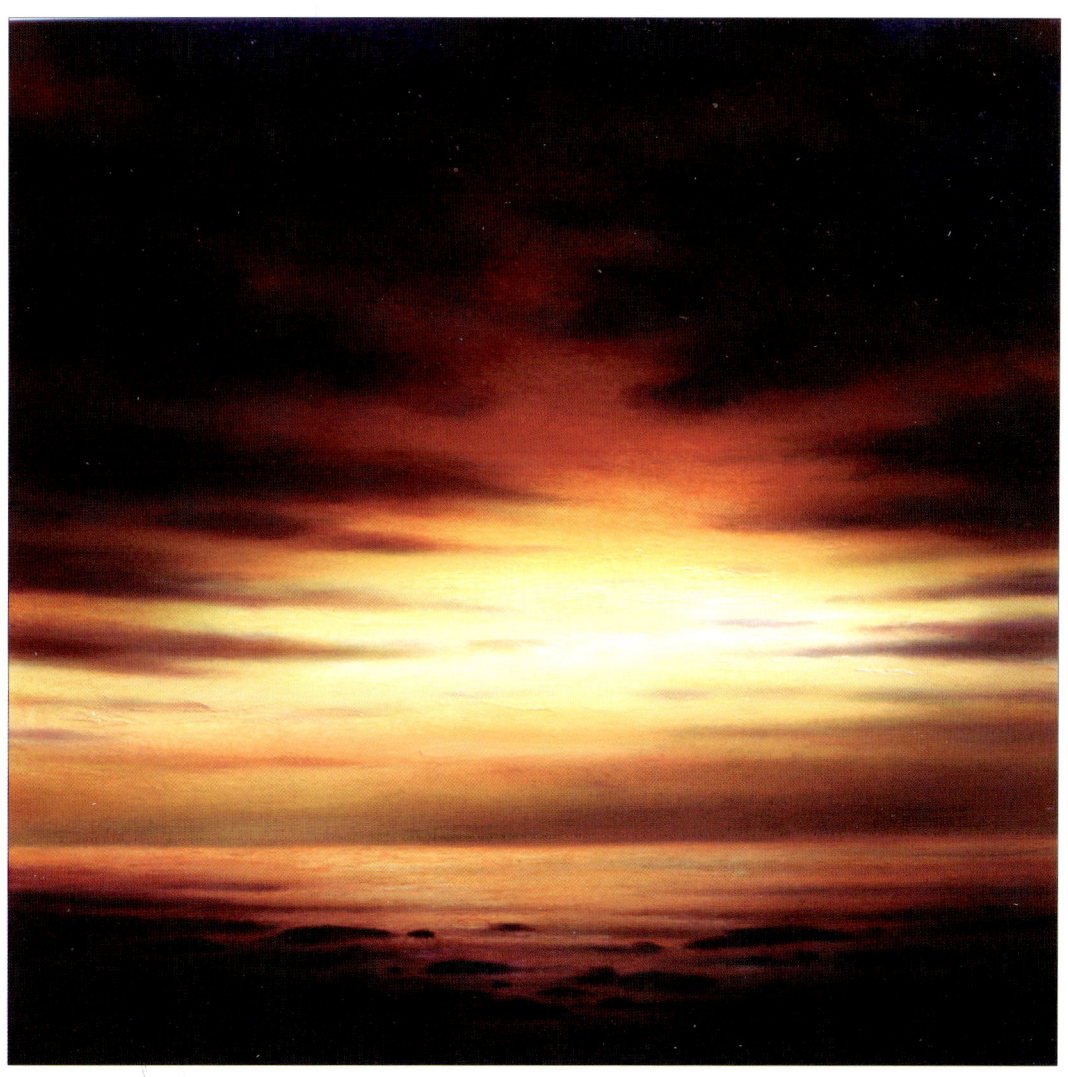

Red Valley
oil on board
82 x 56cm

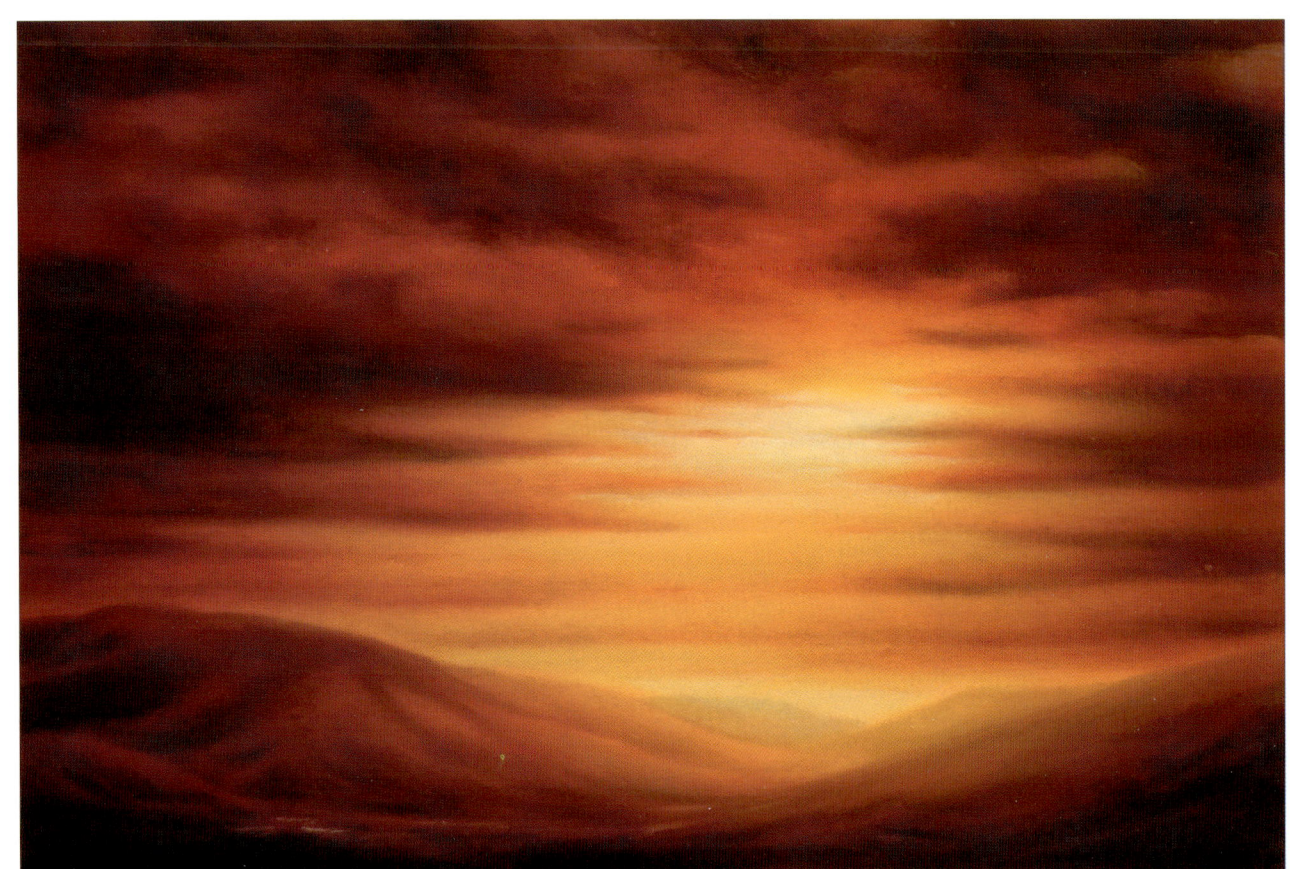

On the Road to Maam
oil on board
35 x 25cm

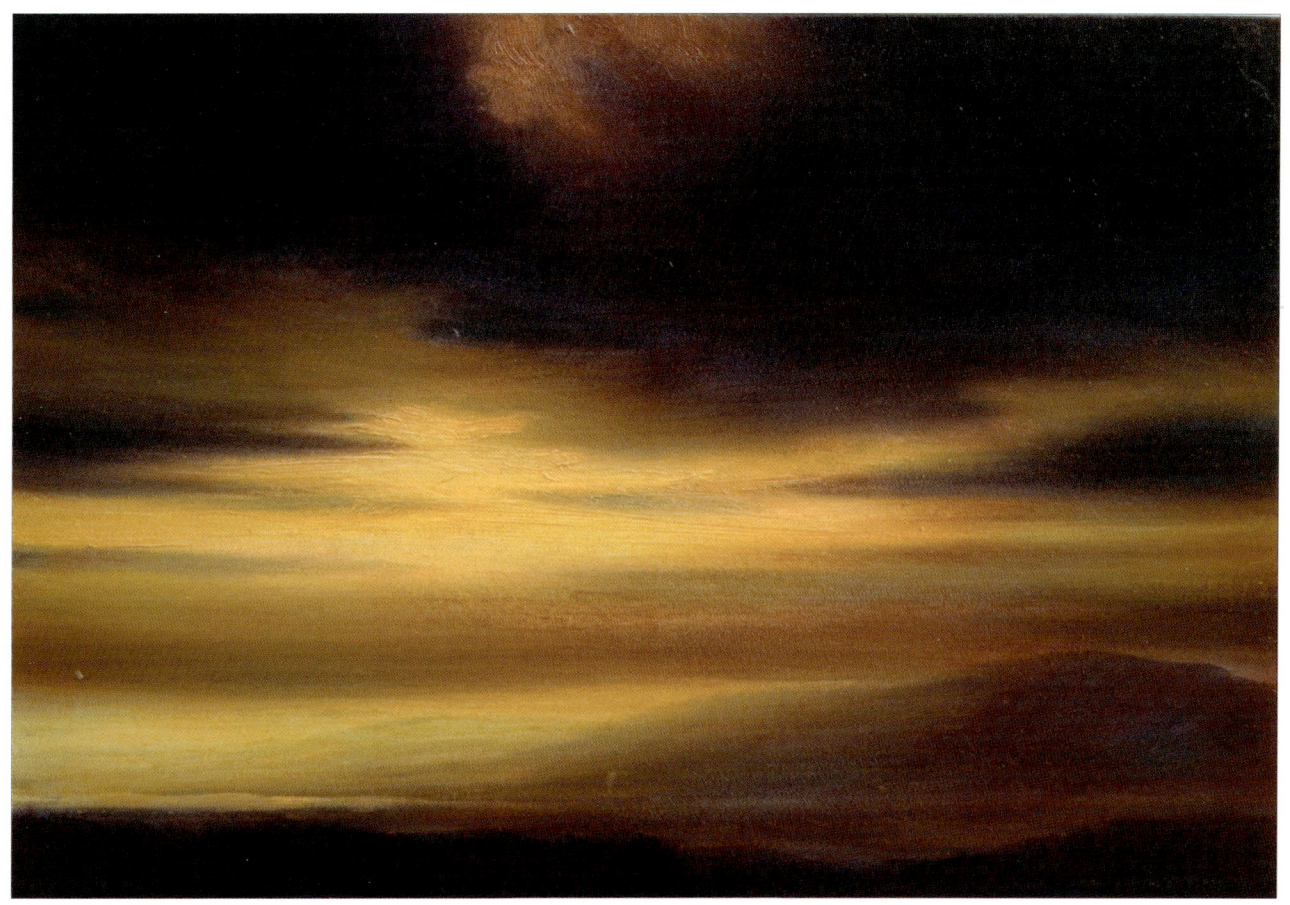

Jim's Vision

Jim's vision is ecstatic
A skyscape sundown lumen
A raft of light, glaze thin bright
A numinous translucence
Running hot red and cold white.
It is as if the canvas
Is lit from within its depths
Sky, a blast of dragon's breath.

We met in London's cold and
Grimy streets, its glittering
Retreats and talked for hours
On that first occasion
Instant friends at first sight then
And now and always too I
Know. A plasterer by trade
He made his paintings with a

Craftsman's care but with the
Daring of an artist's eye. Why
Pickle sheep in tanks when your
Brush preserves the whole wide sky?
Down by the Corrib, Annie –
Wife, son – Tom, and dog Eddie
Six o'clock or more, we have
Been celebrating all night

Here, dear Annie's fortieth
Year. She handles everything
With quiet style, knowing who
Is sad and who is bad, who
Needs to go home now. We take
Whiskey, picnic baskets and
Harmonicas, cameras, warm
Coats, glasses, big smiles, warm hugs,

Poetry and friendship down
To the Corrib Lough at the
Edge of the world. In late morning
Jim and I sip tea in his
Studio full of light, the light
Comes from the paintings as well.
It is because he does not assume
To be extraordinary that he is.

Into the Valley
oil on canvas
108 x 52cm

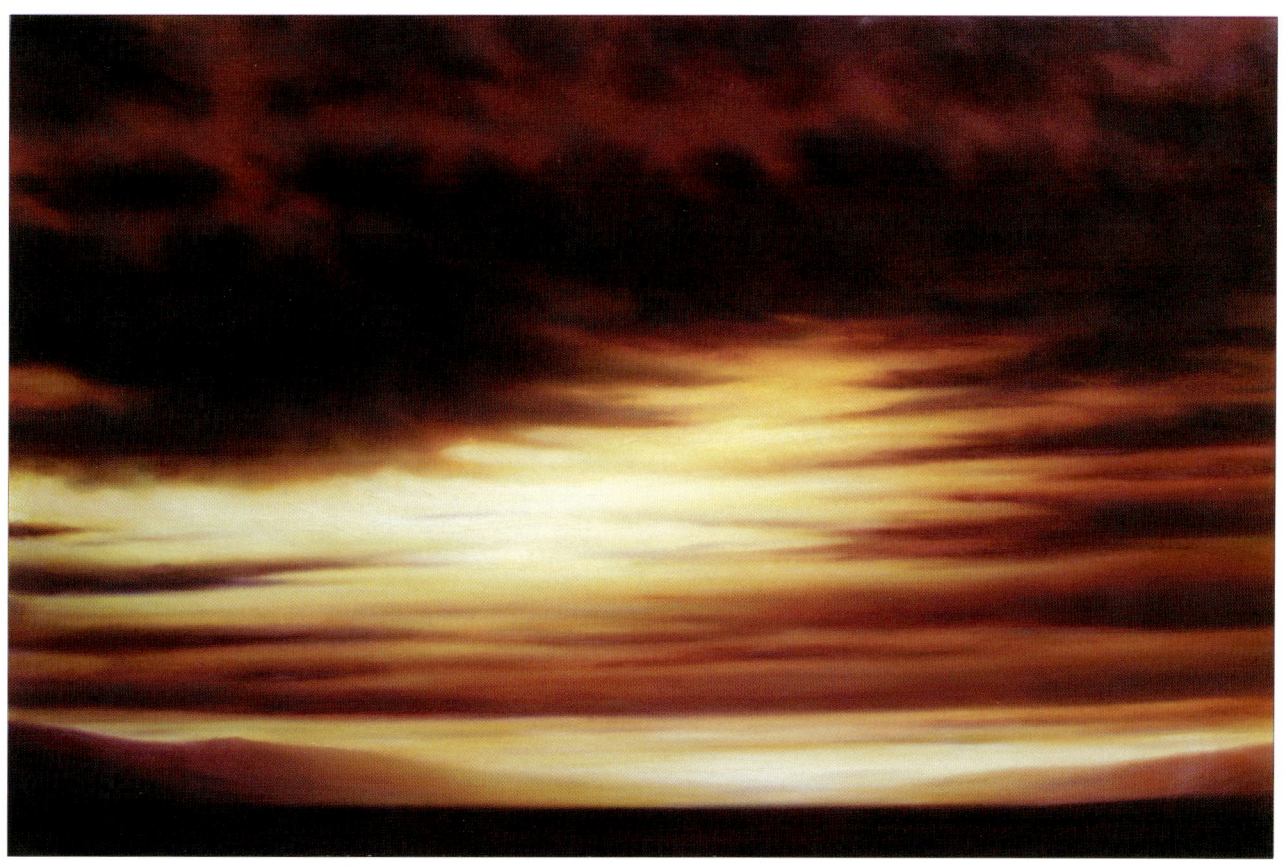

Slieve League
oil on canvas
82 x 56cm

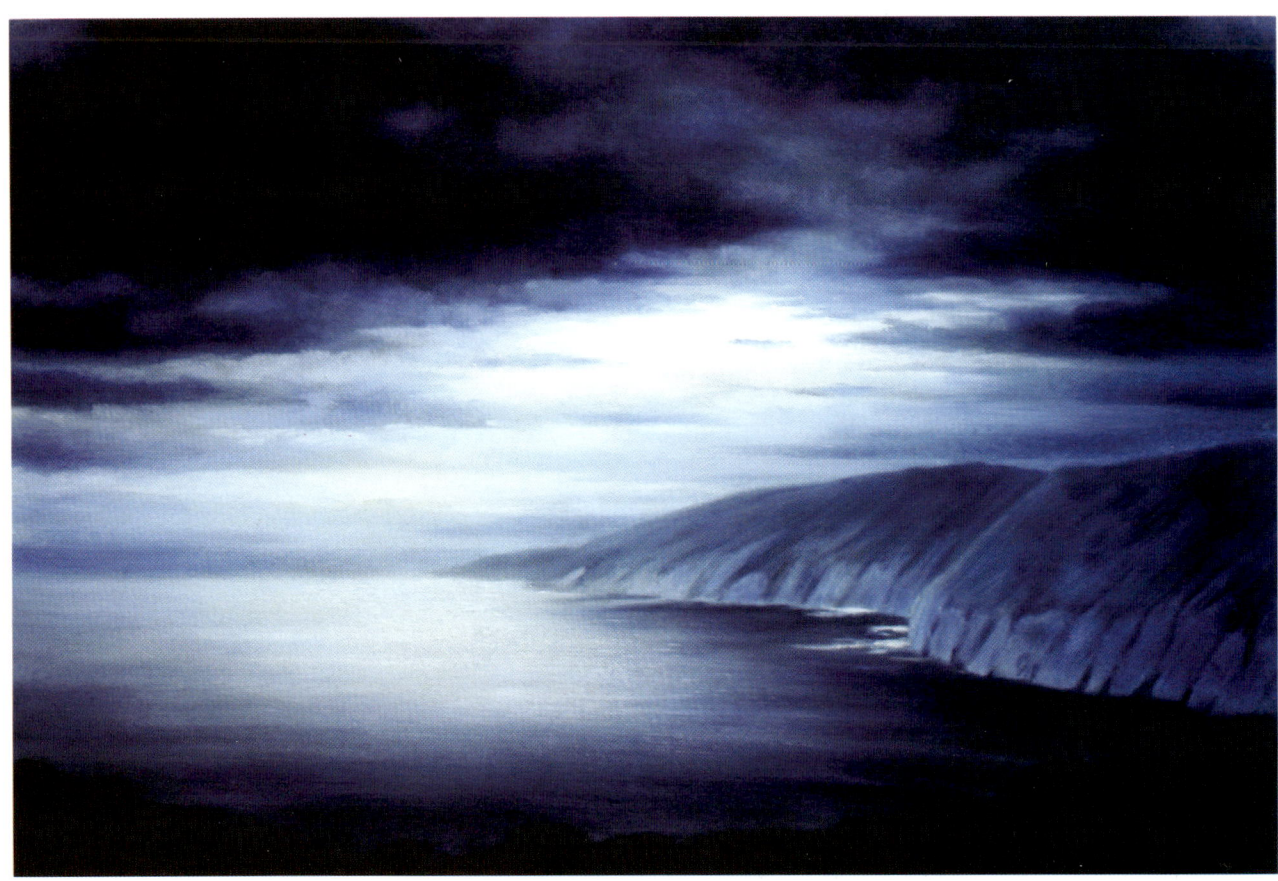

Achill Island
oil on canvas
41 x 41cm

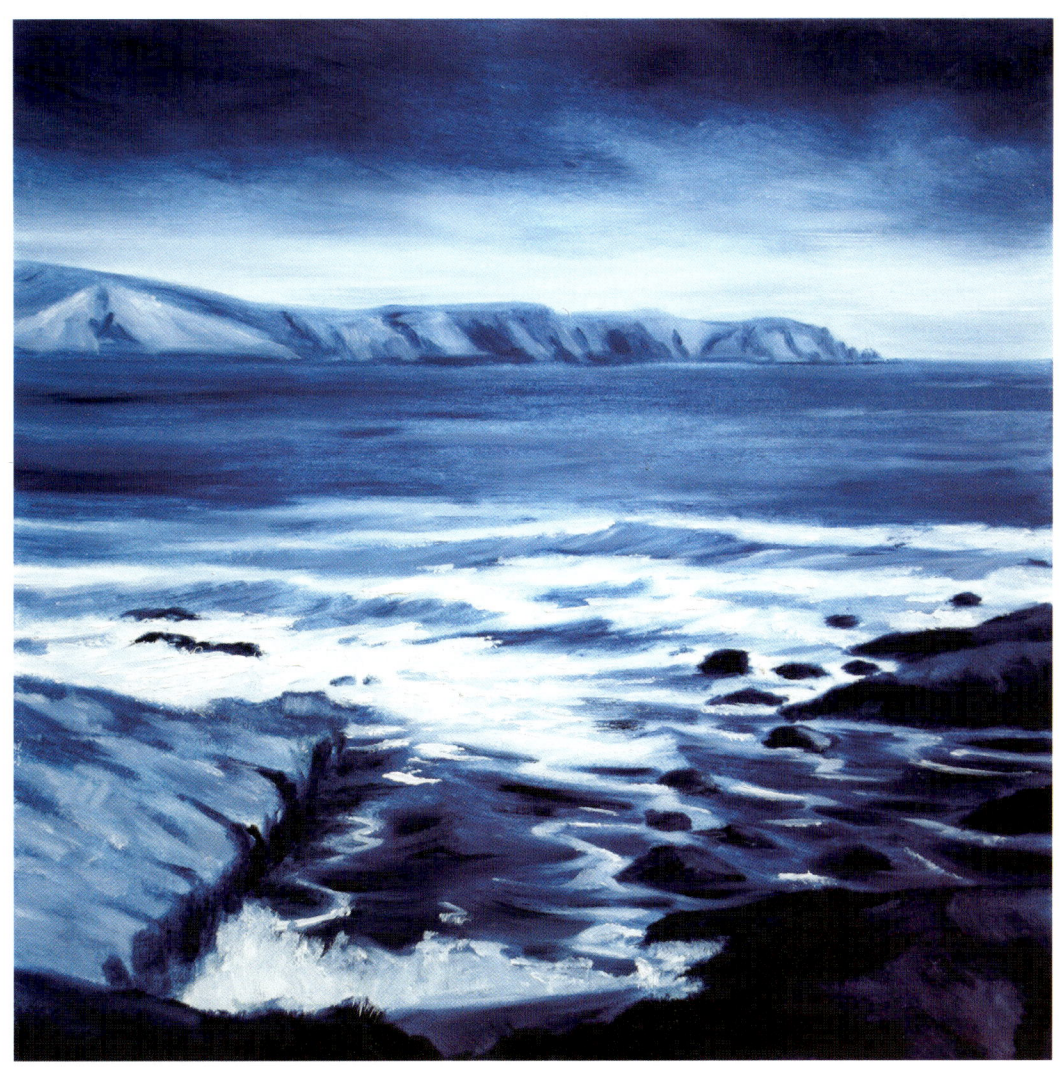

Balindiff Bay
oil on canvas
82 x 52cm

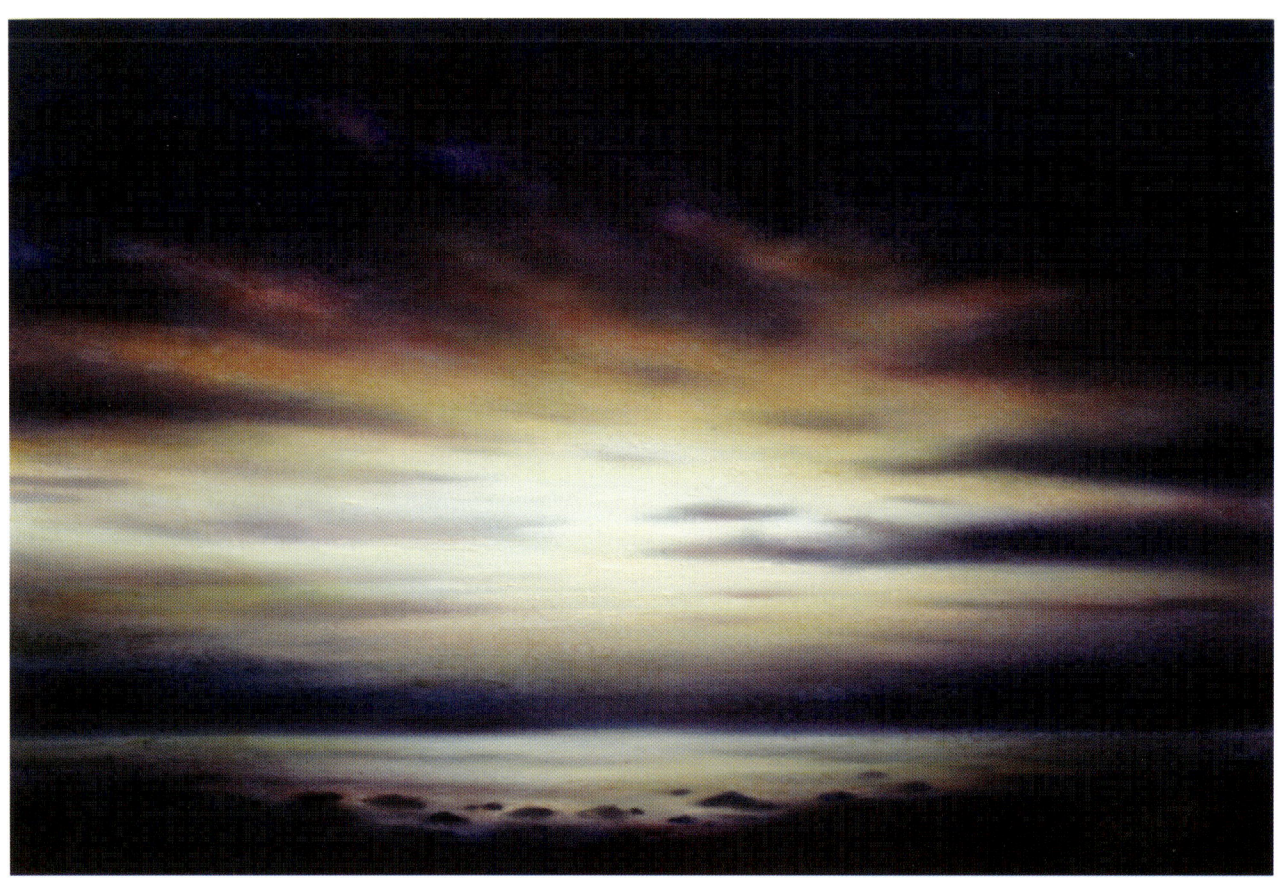

Silver Strand
oil on canvas
41 x 31cm

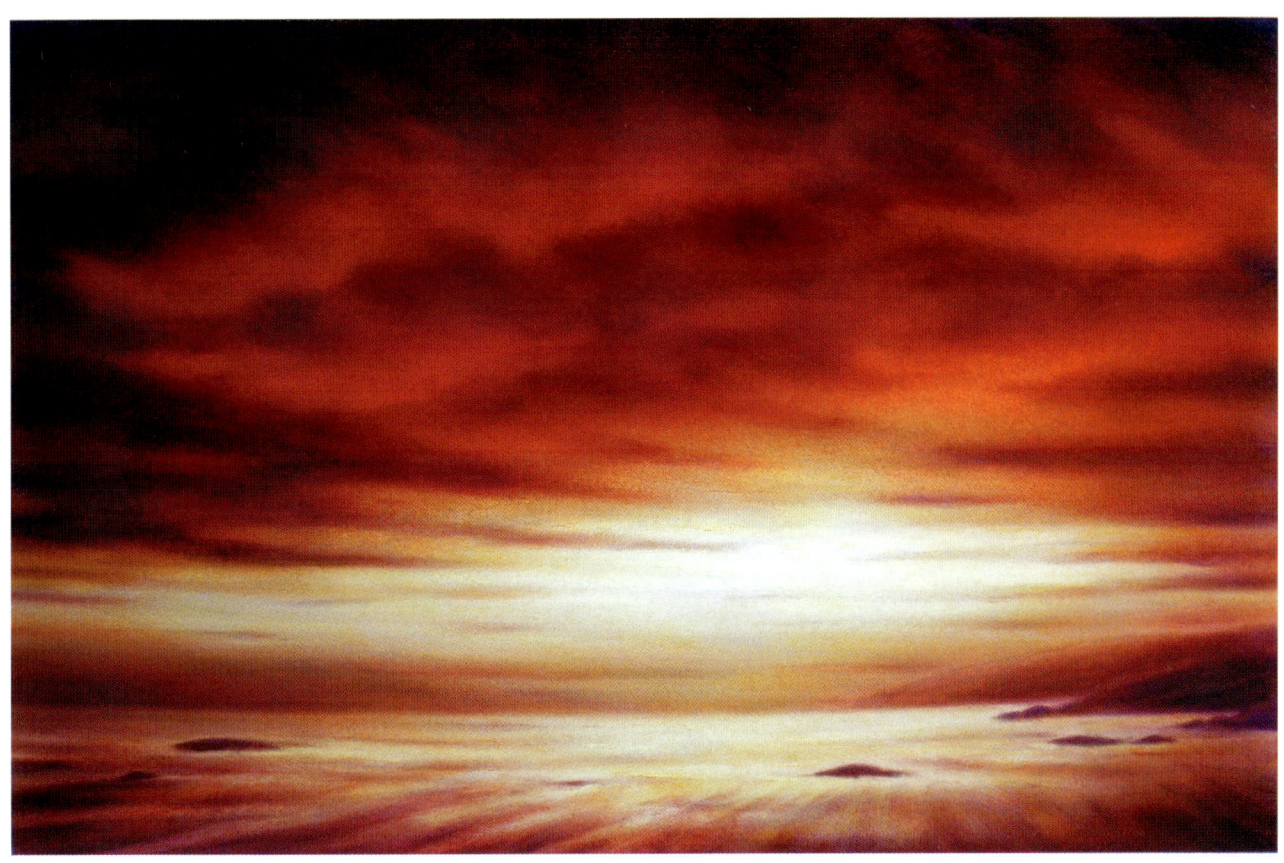

Towards Joyce Country
oil on canvas
100 x 50cm

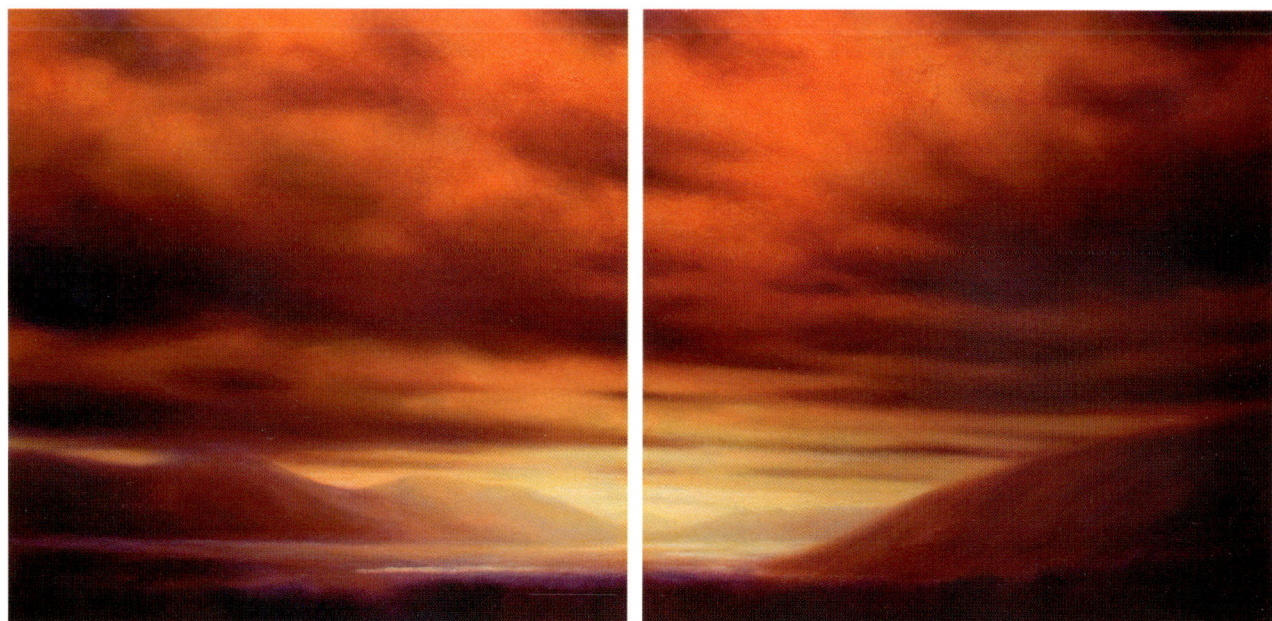

Joyce Country
oil on canvas
51 x 38cm

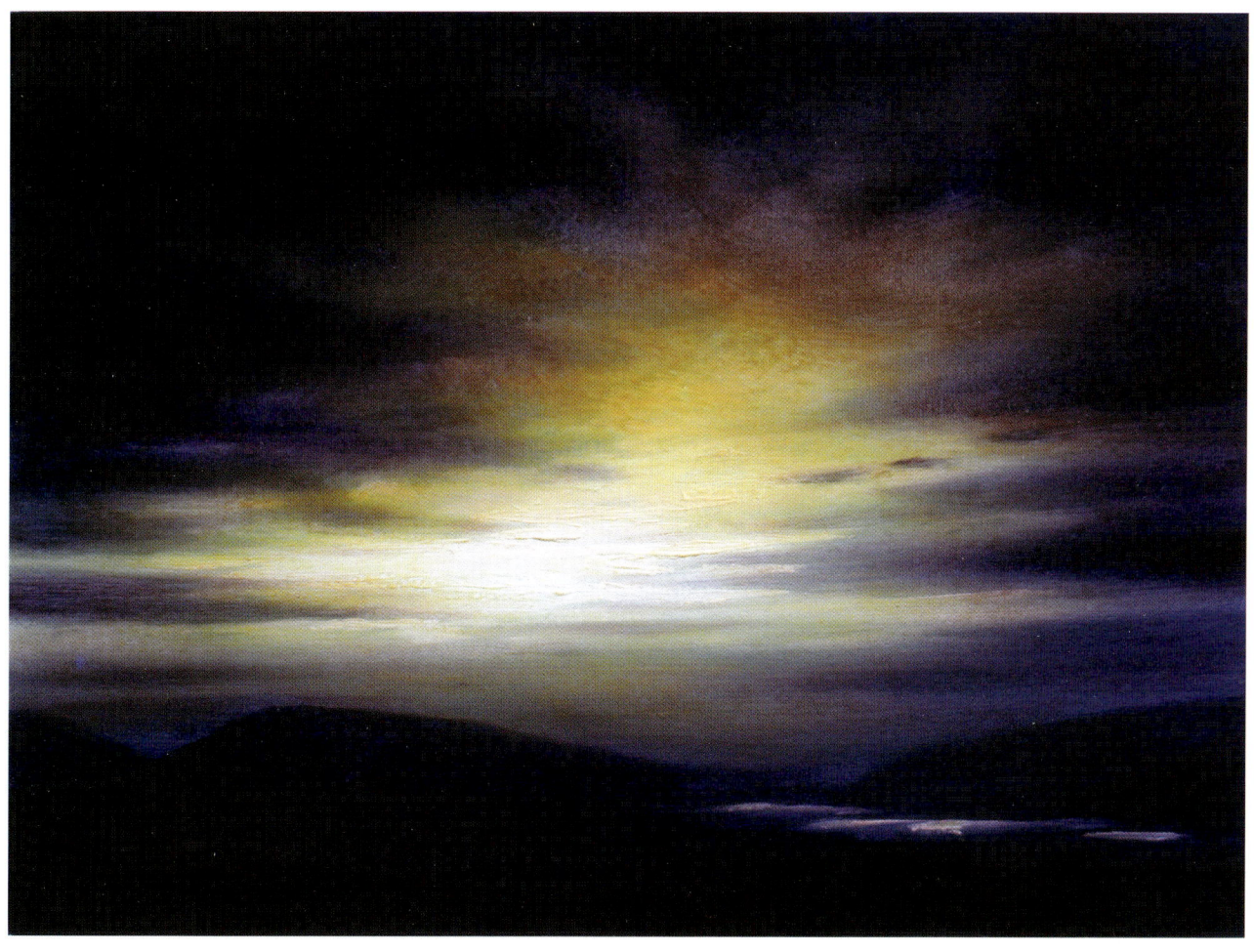

Towards Louisburgh
oil on canvas
56 x 40cm

Dooega Achill Island
oil on canvas
41 x 41cm

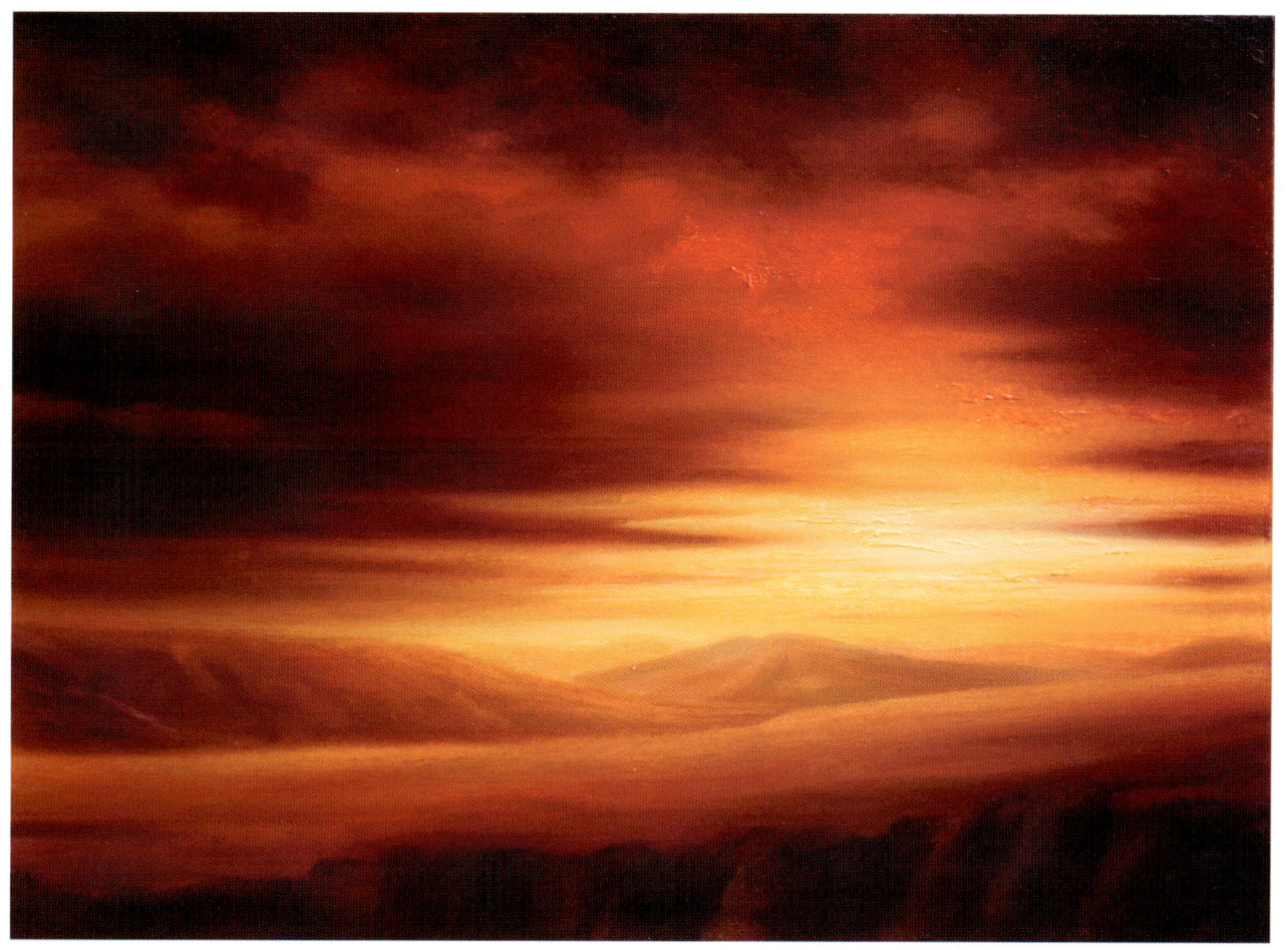

Jouneys End
oil on canvas
122 x 122cm

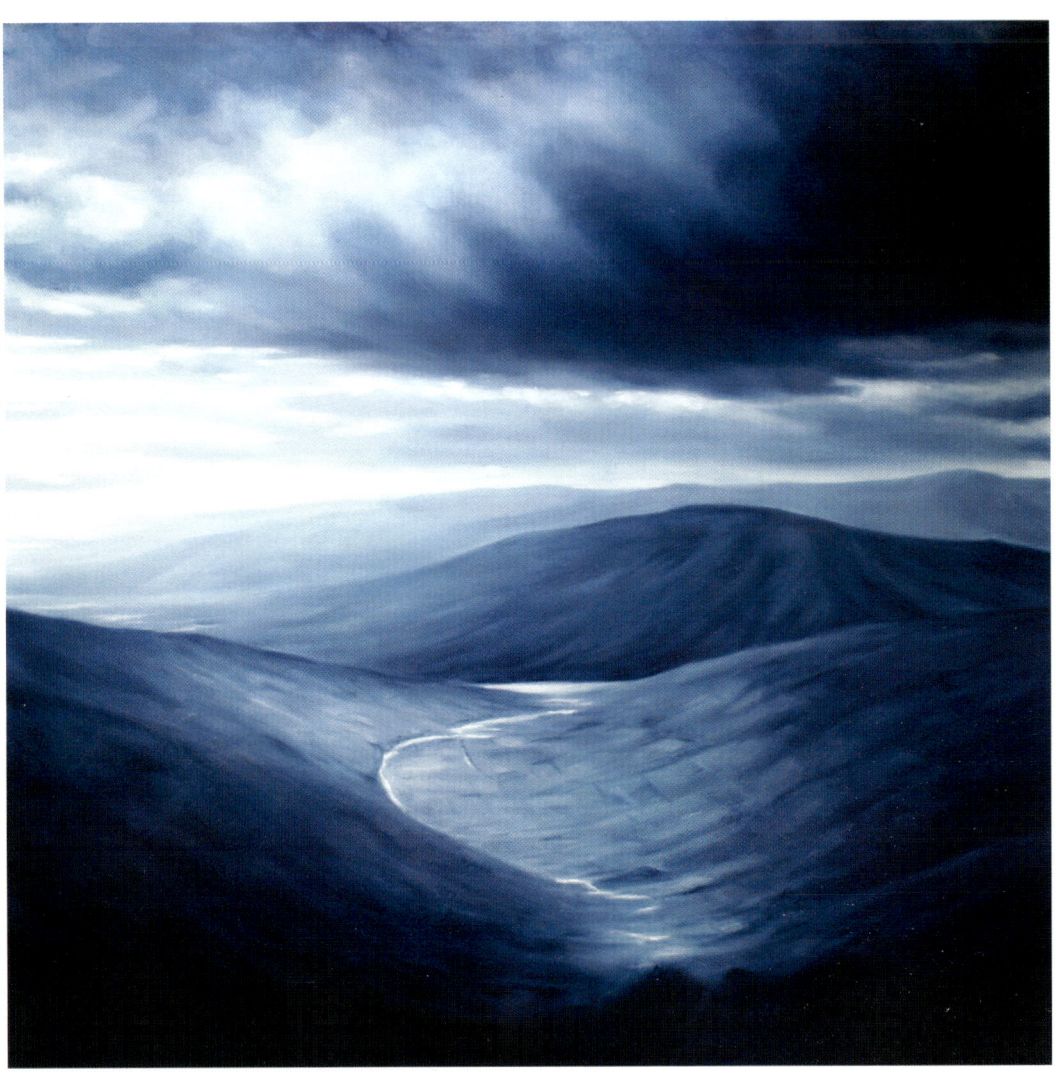

Journey's End

Biography

Jim Kavanagh

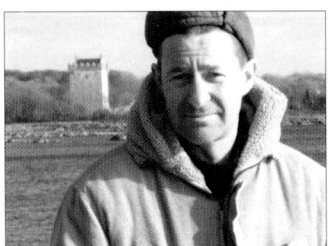

Jim Kavanagh was born in London to Irish parents. He obtained a degree in Fine Art at the University of Middlesex, going on to teach art at third level for a number of years before developing his own art career. In 1994 his work came to the attention of 'Independent Art Promotions' and several exhibitions were organized in London. His semi-abstract and visionary landscapes immediately attracted interest from several leading critics. Due to the success of his exhibitions, he was able to give up teaching and paint full time at his studio in London. The following years he exhibited in Coomb's Contemporary, Bruton Street Gallery and Rebecca Hossack Gallery amongst others, as well as at European art fairs where he is represented by 'Contemporary Irish Art'. He has paintings in several finance companies in the city of London where he was commissioned to do large-scale canvases.

Jim moved to the west of Ireland in 2002 where he continues to paint the landscape which has considerably enhanced his work. He exhibits in Galway, Dublin, London and his work is in corporate and private collections in Ireland, England, Hong Kong and Australia. He also shows his work on an international online gallery called eyestorm.com. He paints haunting shifting sky-scapes where light and colour are fundamental. Early on he was particularly influenced by the vibrant colours of Emile Nolde, as well as the traditions of the romantics such as Turner, combining the influence of Rothko and Tapies whilst employing old master techniques.

Richard Dyer

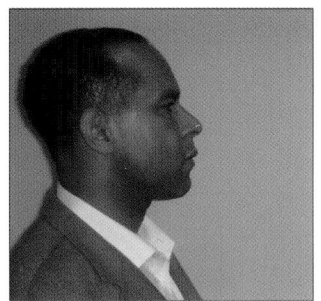

Richard Dyer was born in north London. He studied painting at Winchester School of Art and still makes work alongside his writing. He is News Editor and London Correspondent for *Contemporary* magazine, for which he writes a monthly column on the London artworld; Assistant Editor at *Third Text: Critical Perspectives on Contemporary Art and Culture*; and Art Editor of *Wasafiri*, the magazine of international contemporary writing. He is a Corresponding Editor for *Ambit* literary magazine for which he worked as Assistant Editor for over fifteen years.

Richard is a widely published art critic, reviewer, poet and fiction writer. His critical writing has appeared in *Frieze*, *Flash Art*, *Art Press*, *Third Text*, *Wasafiri*, *The Guardian*, *Time Out*, *Citizen K*, and many other publications and catalogues. His poetry and fiction have been published in *Contemporary*, *Ambit*, *Moving Worlds*, *Victoria*, *Die Ausensites des Elementes*, *Junger Welt*, *Cronica Latina*, *Wasafiri* and *Le Gun*. He has read at events associated with the Galway Literary Festival in 2000 and 2005. In London he has read at the Hackney Literary Festival, the Colony Room Club, Blacks and the French House, all in Soho, and at the Chelsea Arts Club.

Although generally known as an art critic and poet Richard is also a professional blues harmonica player, playing under the title of The Critical Harp. He has played with The Blockheads at Ronnie Scott's in Soho, and Sketch, the Great Eastern Hotel and The Café Royal. He has also played with The Ken Ardley Playboys (artist Bob and Roberta Smith's band) at the Hackney Empire, The Serpentine Gallery and Beconsfield Gallery. He often combines music and poetry in his performances.

His latest publications are *Electronic Shadows: The Art of Tina Kean*, (Black Dog, 2004), with Jean Fisher and Peter Wollen and *Riddled with Light*, on the work of painter Susie Hamilton, (Paul Stolper, 2006). He is currently editing his next collection of poems, *The Romance Engine*.

ISBN 10: 1–903631–69-6
ISBN 13: 978–1–903631–69–0

First published in October 2006 by Arlen House

Arlen House
PO Box 222
Galway
Phone/Fax: 00 353 86 8207617
Email: arlenhouse@gmail.com

Distributed in North America by Syracuse University Press

Syracuse University Press
621 Skytop Road, Suite 110
Syracuse, NY 13244–5290
Phone: 315–443–5534/Fax: 315–443–5545
Email: supress@syr.edu

Photographer: Martina Regan
Designer: Tom Kavanagh
Printed in Ireland

Acknowledgements

Ambit magazine
Alan Hayes
Hazel Hendy
Michael D Higgins
Ria Higgins
Tom Kavanagh
John Killalea
Moving Worlds magazine
Zöe Petersen
Rape Crisis Centre, Galway
Martina Regan
Anne Riordan
Kay Tighe
Josephine Vahey